HOW TO BE AN AWESOME PIANO BAR ENTERTAINER ON CRUISE SHIPS

Gregg Akkerman

Book #2 in the *Awesome Music is Your Business* Series

©2018 by Gregg Akkerman
All rights reserved. Copyright under Berne Copyright Convention, Universal Copyright Convention, and Pan American Copyright Convention. No part of this book may be reproduced, stored in a retrieval system, or transmitted in any form, or by any means, electronic, mechanical, photocopying, recording or otherwise, without the express written consent of the publisher, except in the case of brief excerpts in critical reviews or articles.

Published by RIP Productions
Palm Desert, California 92260
ISBN-13: 978-1-7177-9823-7

DEDICATION

All the devotion to Kathy: my once eleven-year-old playground crush who became the wife of my dreams and fully supports this crazy-love life of ours.

CONTENTS

Acknowledgments 1
Introduction: Being an Awesome Entertainer Is Easier Than You Think 3
Chapter 1: The Piano Bar Entertainer Starter Kit 11
Chapter 2: Getting Your First Gig 35
Chapter 3: Playing Your Gig 51
Chapter 4: Keeping Your Gig 65
Chapter 5: Overview of the Cruise Lines 79
Chapter 6: Awesome Protips 83
Chapter 7: Your Long-Term Career Plan 99
Chapter 8: An Evening in the Life of Piano Dude Gregg 105
Appendix 1: Booking Contacts 109
Appendix 2: Packing List 111
Appendix 3: Song Lists 117
Appendix 4: Arranging Songs 131
Appendix 5: Learning Songs 141
About the Author 149
Review Request 150
Other Books from Gregg Akkerman 151

ACKNOWLEDGMENTS

My abundant appreciation goes out to all those crew mates, peers, friends, cruise-ship guests, and acquaintances who propagated my enlightenment to finish this project of the heart. Specific gratitude to Kathy Akkerman and Roy Mezzapelle for their excellent editorial assistance.

A NOTE ABOUT COVID-19
This book was originally published before the Covid-19 pandemic brought the travel industry to a halt. Slowly, the cruise lines crawled back, but musicians have learned the hard way that we have to be more pro-active about protecting our careers.

The main piece of advice I would give to post-pandemic musicians of all stripes is to always have multiple income streams available. Be sure to diversify your skills including live performance across many genres, in-person or in virtual teaching, publishing, internet influencer, author, technician, tuner, consultant, music director, church band, whatever it takes to pay those bills.

Cruise ship work is awesome but avoid being caught in the next pandemic without any other source of income. In other words, take care of your business and take care of yourself!

—Gregg Akkerman, March 2022

INTRODUCTION: BEING AN AWESOME ENTERTAINER IS EASIER THAN YOU THINK

"Wow, you are really living the dream life." I long ago lost track of how many times I've heard those words from friends, family, and complete strangers. But I won't deny they are true. I make great money, travel to exotic locations around the earth for free, work with talented and attractive people, have food and lodging provided at no cost, receive medical care without being billed, spend my days relaxing in the equivalent of a 5-star hotel resort, and hang out with friends every night being offered free drinks while hearing all my favorite songs. So yes, I see it for the dream life it is. I have the awesome job of being a Piano Bar Entertainer on cruise ships. Want to do what I do? Read on and I'll walk you through it.

The Real Job Description Cruise Ship Companies Won't Tell You

The biggest cruise line in the world officially describes the Piano Bar Entertainer (or simply PBE) as someone who can "deliver high-energy and interactive entertainment to our guests." The general job skills they expect include, "musicality, personality, and unpredictability." Specifically, they cite the following preferred attributes:

- A talented entertainer who demonstrates strong skills as a piano/vocal entertainer
- Repertoire of at least 250 classic piano bar songs, including sing-alongs
- Demonstrated ability to perform completely acoustic (no backing tracks)
- Related performance experience on cruise ships, piano bars and/or dueling piano bars
- Ability to create and lead musical-based games and activities
- Ability to accommodate and learn song requests
- Ability to perform safety functions and pass a pre-employment medical exam
- Fluent in the English language and familiar with North American culture and humor

Don't let any of that list overwhelm or intimidate you. If you're a pianist/vocalist ready to change your life, let me sum up the real PBE job description in a two-word truth bomb: ALCOHOL SALESPERSON. The job of a PBE is to keep butts in seats and drinks in hands. That's it. Nothing more. And if you go into this gig convinced it is something else, you won't last, and you'll likely be miserable before you finally quit or get fired. Extensive music training and performance experience might help (sometimes it gets in the way), but those elements are hardly the most important keys to PBE success like I provide in this book. So if you can let go of romanticized pre-conceptions or the "official" job descriptions and instead embrace the true essence of the PBE gig, you've passed the first test, and the dream life described in the first paragraph is yours for the taking.

Still with me? Alright then, let's talk details and start you on your way.

How Much Money You Will Make

Let's admit it, what you really want to know up front is, "What's the pay?" PBEs are notoriously tight-lipped when it comes to admitting what they make, and I'm sure I'm breaking an unwritten code by sharing the information, but here it is: at the time this book is being written in 2018 a PBE can easily earn $6,000 a month. I'm sure some make more and some certainly make less, but I'm giving you a number that is quite realistic. There is considerable variety in what you can make because of your years of experience, negotiating skills, agency fees, and whether you are allowed a tip jar. Cruise lines that don't allow a tip jar on the piano typically pay a higher salary, so it's easy for you to budget and know what you'll be earning during your contract, and people will still tip you, it just isn't as overt. Cruise lines that allow a tip jar will pay you less salary (low $4,000s a month), but there is literally no cap on what you potentially earn.

So what can you expect to make in tips? Again, PBEs rarely go on the record about such details, and I have learned to be suspicious of the dollar amounts shared by others. On the few occasions tips are discussed, I think it is common for PBEs to greatly inflate the numbers. And to be fair, there is great variety based on where you are sailing and the nationalities of the cruisers. Personally, I have found the best tippers are Americans on Caribbean cruises (tips on west-coast cruises of the U.S. aren't as high for some reason). Europeans, Canadians, and the English typically tip less, and the Aussies hardly at all—it's just not part of their culture like it is in America. All that being said, making $500 a week in tips while in the Caribbean is common enough that you can call anything less a "low" week. But to be clear, I've had weeks where I've barely scraped up $200 while the very next week have been tipped $1,000 in one night by one person! Never knowing for sure who is walking through those piano bar doors each night is part of what makes the job so fascinating.

Keep in mind that whatever your pay is, it includes travel, lodging, food, medical care, a gym membership, and discounts in the ship stores. If you set your life up in a way that you have no bills back home, you can save nearly every dollar you make. This is a powerful life-altering aspect of working on a cruise ship and not to be under-valued. Working a few years at sea can put you financially far ahead compared to working as a musician on land where you're paying for a car, a place to live, various forms of insurance, cable TV, a fitness club, and all your meals. You should also know that the PBE is usually the highest-earning musician on a ship (after tips) because no one else is qualified to be a pianist, lead singer, comedian, game show host, circus manager, and salesperson all wrapped up in one crew member. The PBE position is completely unique on a ship and as such you will be well paid.

Three recent years of daily average PBE income (including salary and tips for all days spent on a ship during each year):
Year A=$215 per day
Year B=$217
Year C=$210

My salary paid by the cruise lines has increased over the above years but sometimes tips have gone down, thus lower overall numbers. Drops may occur because I purposely choose cruise-ship itineraries that are known for lower tips, primarily Alaska, west coast of U.S., and cruises lasting two weeks or longer. The money isn't always as great, but I see some *amazing* places.

Excellent Musicianship Is Optional

As I'll explain in more detail below, I am an exceedingly educated musician, so after the tens of thousands of dollars spent on my schooling, it pains me to admit the fact that you don't have to be an exceptionally good musician to be an awesome PBE. It makes the job easier, but it isn't a prerequisite. **I could perform as a PBE just as successfully without ever having gone to college.**

I'm on a cruise ship as I write this paragraph, and just last night a guest in the piano bar was telling me that on his last cruise the PBE had an awful singing voice and was only a competent pianist, but the room was packed every night. How did he do it? He had a great personality and put on a show based on humor and crowd participation. The guest also shared that on another cruise the PBE was a wonderfully skilled concert pianist who played to an empty room. Why? He never looked up from the keyboard or made any attempt to connect with guests. My point is not to dismiss the usefulness of formal music education but to emphasize that the real difference between a good and awesome PBE is not musicianship, it's showmanship.

If you are already a highly trained musician, great, you will make use of those skills daily as a PBE, but don't think it will excuse you from being an entertainer. And if you currently have limited music training, don't let it be a deal breaker for you. Start studying for the long-term, but put considerably more attention on your stage show (discussed in depth later) in order to win over the crowd. The reality is that you'll always get a bigger crowd response from playing a campy song that makes everyone laugh than from playing a note-perfect performance of your favorite jazz or progressive rock artist. In a piano bar, like it or not, Chuck Berry's "My Ding-a-ling" delivered with a smile will always win over "Spain" from Chick Corea or "Tom Sawyer" from Rush, no matter how well you play. Not only should you accept that fact, but take advantage of it on a regular basis. While the crowd is giggling over Berry's cheeky lyrics, those of you with training can throw in an 8-bar interlude taken from your favorite Haydn piano sonata, Keith Emerson excerpt, or Herbie Hancock riff. You keep your chops up, and the tip jar stays busy. Win-win. Those without a lot of technique can play with one hand for a verse while putting the other hand in your lap and telling the crowd, "I'm playing with my ding-a-ling right now." You are actually making a strength out of a weakness and winning the crowd with personality over musicianship. You will need to be clever, but it can be done.

The best solution for the long-term is to have a great stage show and enough music training to make the job easier. Being able to listen to a requested song a couple times, download the lyrics, and perform it the next night in any key with limited rehearsal is a great way to increase your tips, but that only comes from an abundance of ear training and application of music theory. If that goal seems years away, you'll need more gimmicks, funny glasses, silly bits like the "Baby Shark" song, conversational skills, drink toasts, and crowd participation games compared to another PBE who can fill the time with more songs and longer instrumental sections. I'll give more suggestions on developing your stage show in Chapter 3.

The Demand for Awesome PBEs Is Higher Than the Supply

At first glance, it would seem that supply and demand would work against musicians looking to work as a PBE. There are roughly 100 cruise ships in the world that need pianists, and you might ask, "I'm not one of the 100 best in the world so how can I ever expect to get hired?" But that's not how the numbers work. One ship might use 6-8 pianists each year because each contract lasts 2-4 months. With only that adjustment, the demand for PBEs goes up considerably. But the biggest impact on supply verses demand for PBEs is turn over. Frankly, most PBEs (along with all cruise ship musicians) don't last beyond one or two contracts. Perhaps the job isn't what they thought because they didn't do the research, or were misled by an agent who didn't ask enough questions. For others, being away from family is just too stressful. Sometimes health issues get in the way. Then there are some PBEs who get fired for various bad behaviors or incompetence (it definitely happens). For all those reasons, there is enough turnover that if you want to get hired as a PBE and follow the advice in this book, you're nearly certain to get an offer. The demand verses supply is in your favor, and because you've done the research and know what you're getting into, you'll likely work for as long as you want.

My Background

So, what makes me the expert on how to be an awesome PBE? That's a fair question. I've been a performing pianist since the mid-1980s, have always made a living as a musician or music educator, and have spent years doing the exact things I'm talking about in this book. This is not hypothetical theory I'm giving you; it is battle-tested wisdom straight from the trenches of the cruise ship piano bars where I still slug it out on a regular schedule. I have two advanced university degrees in music including a doctorate, but I use very little of that education compared to what I've learned sitting at a piano bench night after night interacting with the people around me.

I love reading books on music theory (I'm a geek that way), but knowing what pivot chord to use when modulating between unrelated keys is useless when a drunk guest from Phoenix is yelling at me to play "Sweet Caroline" even though I just finished it. They don't teach how to handle that in college my friends.

Being able to sing and play with confidence is truly important, but street-smarts is what keeps you having a good time and out of trouble. Ultimately, being a PBE is a fabulous job full of surprises, challenges, financial rewards, and satisfying moments, and after years of navigating through my career as a musician, I want to pass that information on to others who can now skip some of the hard lessons and get to the good stuff a little faster. Let's make it happen!

CHAPTER 1: THE PIANO BAR ENTERTAINER STARTER KIT

Okay, you're ready to attack your goal of becoming an awesome cruise ship Piano Bar Entertainer–excellent! What you need is a PBE starter kit with all the basic tools of the trade. Some of the tools are actual physical items, while others are skills you must acquire or hone. After you've got your starter kit and demo package together we can begin the process of preparing for and landing your first gig. First things first.

Piano Skills: the Minimum and Optimum

How skilled a piano player do you need to be to become an awesome cruise ship piano bar entertainer? In all honesty I would say, "good but not great." Think of it as a numbers game and your goal is to get a total score of 100 points from three categories: pianist, singer, and entertainer. If you're only at 20 as a pianist, then you'll need to make up 80 points by being one heck of a singer and entertainer. It can be done but may take a while to bolster those other two areas. Frankly, it's easier to improve your skills as an entertainer, so that's the area you should spend most of your time at first. Improving your skills as a pianist and vocalist will become your long-term plan so that eventually you feel an equilibrium in all three categories. But it's not unusual that experienced PBEs are stronger in one area over the others. In fact, it may be useful to identify yourself as one of the following three types of PBE:

1. **Pianist-Singer**: this is a PBE with strong piano skills who picked up singing as a convenient afterthought. Piano teachers and keyboardists in cover bands often fall into this group. This is the category I originally placed myself.

2. **Singer-Pianist**: this is a PBE with an excellent singing voice who picked up enough piano skills along the way to act as their own accompanist. Many voice teachers and musical theater performers fall into this group.

3. **The Double Threat:** this is the rare PBE with a great voice who can work the piano with ease. I have spent years improving my vocals so that I feel I've earned this status, but it was a long-term effort, and along the way I leaned heavily on being a pianist-singer.

Did you notice that "entertainer" was not included in the above three classifications? That's because it's mandatory you have or develop excellent showmanship no matter which category you fall in. If you only want to play background music without much crowd interaction, that is not a PBE, that is a cocktail pianist and a totally different gig that doesn't pay as much and is becoming rarer on cruise ships. You would be much wiser over the long term to focus on developing your PBE skills and being able to work as a cocktail pianist when the occasion arises.

Now that you've assigned yourself to a PBE category, let's set a baseline of the pianist skill set you should have as a *minimum* and see how you rate.

The Minimum Piano Skills:

You know at least a dozen songs that you can play and sing at the same time, you don't get overly nervous playing in front of others, even strangers compliment your performance skills, and of course your friends and family think you're fabulous.

You have enough hand independence that your left hand can comfortably play completely different patterns than the right hand.

You read music without constantly staring back and forth between the page and your hands. This skill will allow you to keep your eyes up and connect with guests. Pianists look at the keys. Entertainers look at the crowd.

You must, must, MUST know how to play all the basic three- and four-note chords in your right hand in any inversion in all keys. It's not enough that you can write them down for a music theory test. You have to be able to play them. This includes: major, minor, diminished, augmented, suspended, major 7th, dominant 7th, minor 7th, minor 7th flat 5, diminished 7th, and 7th suspended). If this is a weakness for you, consult YouTube for video tutorials and do one key a week (I've posted some videos myself on the subject). In three months the problem is solved forever. This is a non-negotiable skill so get started.

You can make a simple arrangement from of a lead sheet. Lead sheets are sheet music with only a melody (usually in treble clef) and chord symbols—you provide the unwritten accompaniment. This is why you must know all your chords in inversions. A PBE has hundreds, if not thousands, of songs ready to go on their tablet, and lead sheets are one of the ways to reduce a song to one page. Full-sized sheet music is unwieldly and restrictive. You DO NOT want to be turning pages during a performance.

You can perform a simple arrangement by looking at a song sheet. Song sheets are simply the lyrics with chord symbols written above the words so you know when to change chords. They are quite common with worship bands. There is no sheet music, so you create the entire arrangement on your own (see Appendix 4 for help with creating arrangements). Song sheets can almost always fit on one page and make the life of a PBE much easier. Most of the songs in my repertoire are in song-sheet form.

You memorize many of your songs to the point where you seldom need to glance at the song sheet or lead sheet. Free yourself from full sheet music as soon as possible because page turning and locked-in arrangements are an untenable distraction. You need the flexibility of one-page sheets that allow you to jump around at will, insert or delete sections, and skip to the ending or extend the final chorus as needed. Spontaneity of this sort is a big part of being a PBE. I might consult sheet music when I'm first learning a song and creating my own arrangement, but once that's done, I never look at it again.

If you've got the above skills in hand, good for you! If not, you've got your homework for the next several months of your life. Focus mostly on learning chords and making simple arrangements of tunes you already know by heart. Start with "Happy Birthday" and build up from there. See Appendix 4 for more tips on making your own arrangements.

Now let's consider the *optimum* skills you should aspire to have as a pianist.

The Optimum Piano Skills:

You should also be able to improvise or "solo" over basic rock songs like "Great Balls of Fire," "Johnny B. Good," and "Route 66" while still maintaining a steady beat. This allows you to lengthen arrangements so that you don't have to sing or talk as much. Protecting your voice while working as a PBE for weeks and months is crucial. Start by trying to imitate the solos on the original recordings or even just playing the vocal melody on the piano as an interlude. Little by little, add embellishments with grace notes, arpeggios, or completely new melodies based on the chords and their related scales. Playing longer instrumental sections is also very helpful during sets that are lightly attended and quiet. Rest your voice whenever possible.

You should be able to play basic songs in any key. Transposing songs to new keys has saved my butt countless times. Just this week I was performing with a very tired voice that I need to protect because my contract still has 6 weeks left, so I played several songs in lower keys than usual. Secondly, there are lots of singers working on the ship with you who might come by the piano bar and you'll want to have them sit in for a couple of songs. Last night, the singer from the rock band came to the piano bar on his break and asked to sing "Dream On" from Aerosmith in the original key instead of the lower key I use. Guests loved it, the singer got to strut his stuff, and I got to rest my voice. We all came out ahead. This wouldn't have happened if I only knew how to play in one key. I am able to transpose most my songs by thinking of all the chords as Roman numeral like I, IV, and V. That way the chords become independent of any one key and it's easier to shift between them. Again, YouTube has hundreds of videos to help with this. Digital pianos can transpose for you, but don't count on always having that feature available. Be safe and learn how to transpose "old school."

You can learn songs equally as well from sheet music or by ear. I find that it's faster to learn songs by ear than from sheet music. There's no time lost learning a sheet-music arrangement, transposing it to a key you can sing, and then converting everything into an arrangement that actually works for solo piano with vocals. How many times have you spent hours learning a sheet-music arrangement only to feel that it doesn't sound like the recording everyone knows? When learning by ear, you're making an appropriate and accurate arrangement in your key from the very beginning. It may take you a while to develop a good "ear," but it's well worth the effort. I start by listening for the bass instrument because it is usually playing the root of each chord. I build up from there to determine the exact chord type. The more songs you learn by ear, the more patterns you start to recognize, making the process easier each time. One of the most important things that ever happened in my music education was joining a cover band at age 18 and being handed recordings of 50 songs (no sheet music) with only two weeks to learn. There's nothing like a paying gig to motivate you to learn new skills that will be used the rest of your life.

You should learn how to create your own lead sheets in notation software like Finale. Even though this last item isn't about playing the piano, it is quite useful to your growth as a pianist. If you desperately prefer lead sheets over song sheets (at least at first), you'll want to make your own rather than pay someone else to do it for you. You basically enter an existing lead sheet or the treble-clef melody with chord symbols from existing sheet music into the software, transpose as needed, fit it on one page, save as a PDF file, and load it on your tablet. About 25% of my repertoire is in lead-sheet form. Although I mostly use song sheets, I often notate song introductions or interludes and copy just those measures into my song-sheet documents (in Microsoft Word) as an image before saving it as a PDF. For songs I only play on rare occasion, having the first 8 bars notated gets me started smoothly and then I am good to go creating my own arrangement from there.

Vocal Skills: the Minimum and Optimum

How good of a vocalist do you need to be to become an awesome cruise ship PBE? Similar to what you read concerning the pianist side of the equation, I would say, "sort of good." Singing is the most obvious skill that piano bar guests will notice about your musicianship. On a scale of one to ten, most guests can't tell the difference between a pianist who is a five from an eight. But apply those same ratings to a singer and the difference is clear even to the non-musicians in the room. Therefore, it is far easier to make a strong first impression by being a better singer than pianist, but even PBEs with ragged vocal skills can be very successful and well-liked. Like we learned above, if your goal as a performer is to be operating at a score of 100 and your vocals are the weak link, you'll have to make up for it first as an entertainer and secondly as a pianist. But maybe you're not even sure where you rate as a singer, so let's talk about the difference between the minimum and optimum qualifications.

The Minimum Vocal Skills:

You are greatly familiar with American pop music covering many decades, and constantly find yourself singing along with recordings.

You already sing in public on occasion as a member of a band, worship team, choir, or community theater.

You are able to sing on pitch and sustain your notes. This is all about breath control. If you don't know about diaphragmatic support, look it up because it will instantly improve a wimpy, breathy voice and keep you on pitch. This one act completely turned me around as a singer.

You have a wide enough vocal range to sing the popular songs guests expect. This doesn't mean you have to match Michael Jackson, Steve Perry, or Lady Gaga note for note; as a baritone vocalist, I certainly don't. But if the melody of the song has a one-and-a-half-octave range, you'll need at least that same range no matter how low you transpose the key. There are plenty of great songs out there with narrow ranges (i.e., Jimmy Buffet, Van Morrison, Zac Brown, and many country hits) so focus on those first, but try to increase your range over the long term so you can add more variety to your repertoire. Song variety leads to happy guests, more tips, and increased alcohol sales (lest we forget the true point of the job).

You have enough vocal endurance to get through four hours a night (sometimes with no break), six days a week, for two to four months straight. Until you've done it, you simply can't imagine the toll this amount of singing takes on a voice. I go to great lengths to keep my voice in shape between contracts, but every time I start on a new ship my voice goes into shock during the first week. I can only imagine the breakdown I would experience if I wasn't working to keep my voice healthy. To build endurance you need to sing hours every day leading up to your first contract including a regimen of exercises that will help develop good breath control and expand your range. And when you're on the gig, you need to sing vocal warm-up exercises every day. I have been doing this job for years and still take at least 30 minutes in my cabin each night to get the voice warmed up. I've heard other PBEs say, "I don't do warm ups. I just sing easy songs for the first half hour." That doesn't work when a guest slaps down $20 in the first five minutes of your show and says, "Please play 'Don't Stop Believing' for my wife's birthday before we leave for our dinner reservation." If you're not already warmed up, singing songs like that can damage your voice and leave you waiting for days to recover. It's not worth the risk, so plan to be warmed up before your gig starts.

You limit alcohol consumption. This is a tough one for many PBEs out there. You will learn early in your PBE career that if you want to, you can drink for free all night. Guests love to buy the PBE whatever he or she is drinking. And the next night when you walk in, you might see a drink waiting for you on the piano, complements of an appreciative guest. That's the good life, right? Nope. Pouring alcohol on your vocal cords is the last thing they need to stay healthy. You need water or maybe tea to keep your voice hydrated, not booze. Anyone who says, "a shot will loosen your voice up" is not a professional singer who's in it for the long run. The more likely result of you having a couple drinks is that you feel over-confident and start singing too loud and reaching for notes well beyond your range. The next morning you'll say, "I don't know why I'm so hoarse." Sure you do. Secondly, crew members are technically not allowed to drink at all while on the clock. But it's a well-known fact that security and supervisors look the other way when it comes to the PBE, right until the moment they don't. You drink for weeks during your shows with no problem, and then one night an officer is waiting outside the piano bar ready to give you a breathalyzer test. If it tests positive you will find yourself being sent home on short notice, perhaps never knowing the real reason someone wanted you gone. Stay healthy and keep your gig; cut out the booze while performing.

Optimum Vocal Skills:

You should be employing vowel replacement and vibrato to higher notes as ways to reduce vocal stress. For instance, "ah" become "uh," and "oo" becomes "oh" as you sing higher in your range. Little changes like this can make a substantial difference over the length of a contract.

Start using consonant replacements so you aren't singing so many harsh sounds throughout the night. There are lots of wonderful suggestions to be found on YouTube to help you soften the sounds of letters like k, p, and t. For example, the bridge to Frank Sinatra's "That's Life" is, "I've been a puppet, a pauper, a pirate, and poet, a pawn and a king," but can be sung as, "I've been a bubb-ed, a bauber, a birade, a boh-ed, a bawn and a ging." You wouldn't do this for a studio recording, but it works fine for a live performance. Making these kinds of changes throughout your show reduces vocal stress, and if you are subtle about it and the crowd has been drinking, they won't notice a thing.

You should be developing a strong head voice and mixed voice. This expanded range will allow you to add more interesting and challenging songs to your repertoire to keep guests pleased and keep yourself from getting bored with a limited song list.

I want to share that one of my PBE peers has gone on the record saying he wasn't a strong pianist or singer when he started the job and yet he quickly became the darling of the cruise ship piano bars and guests couldn't stop raving about him. At first, he put all his focus on guest engagement and winning over the crowd with humor and ongoing banter. Behind the scenes he kept practicing piano and working on vocals so that these days those weaknesses rarely show and he has a much more balanced presentation. He is living proof that as long as you have the minimum skills listed above, you can find a way to be an awesome piano bar entertainer.

Repertoire

The next item to organize in your PBE starter kit is repertoire, or to put it another way, all the songs you could potentially perform on a gig. A question I'm often asked by aspiring PBEs is "how many songs do I need to know?" There are several different answers floating around. I have had piano bar guests tell me they have seen PBEs who hand out a list of 100 songs and say, "I don't play any songs not on the list." The PBE job description from a prominent cruise line says they expect you know at least 250 songs. When I worked my first cruise ship job the booking agent suggested I have 300 songs. On a Facebook discussion among a group of PBEs the question of "how many songs do you know" was asked and answers ranged from a few hundred to over two thousand.

What this all means is that there isn't a perfect answer. But for me personally, I recommend not showing up for your first PBE gig with less than 200 songs ready to play. Even then, you will quickly wish you knew more. I remember when I finally got to 300 songs and thought, "Whew, I can relax now." Wrong. The requests kept coming for songs that I really should have known, so the list kept growing. I'm well over 1,500 songs now and added another 25 in the last month. It never ends. I really don't mind constantly adding to my song list because it keeps me engaged as a musician and adds an extra spark of interest when I perform new material.

Maybe you're thinking, "I'll never get a thousand songs learned!" Don't panic. I'm going to give you a list of 50 songs to get you started that will be your go-to songs the rest of your career. With just these 50 songs you could hypothetically get through an evening without playing anything the crowd didn't enjoy. So here it is, the 50 songs you *must* know to be an awesome cruise ship PBE, starting with the "Big-10:"

1. "Sweet Caroline" by Neil Diamond
2. "Brown-eyed Girl" by Van Morrison
3. "Don't Stop Believing" by Journey
4. "Margaritaville" by Jimmy Buffett
5. "Piano Man" by Billy Joel
6. "New York, New York" by Frank Sinatra
7. "Friends in Low Places" by Garth Brooks
8. "Joy to the World" by Three Dog Night
9. "American Pie" by Don McLean
10. "Bad Leroy Brown" by Jim Croce

These ten songs are your bread and butter and will be played most every night, some of them more than once. They will never let you down so learn them, memorize them, and love them.

Protip: seldom play any of the Big-10 without a request (preferably with money) because you'd essentially be giving a song away instead of allowing guests to feel it's being played just for them.

There could be any number of substitutions among the 40 songs on the list below, but I think even the most experienced PBE would have to admit that you can't go wrong with these choices:

11. "All My Exes Live in Texas" by George Strait
12. "Bennie and the Jets" by Elton John
13. "Blueberry Hill" by Fats Domino
14. "Bohemian Rhapsody" by Queen (if this song is over your abilities, replace it with "Fat Bottom Girls" or another Queen classic)
15. "Build Me Up Buttercup" by the Foundations
16. "Can't Help Falling in Love" by Elvis Presley
17. "Can't Take My Eyes Off of You" by Tom Jones
18. "Come Sail Away" by Styx
19. "Crazy" by Patsy Cline
20. "Crocodile Rock" by Elton John
21. "Dancing Queen" by ABBA
22. "Dock of the Bay" by Ottis Redding
23. "Family Tradition" by Hank Williams, Jr.
24. "The Gambler" by Kenny Rogers
25. "Great Balls of Fire" by Jerry Lee Lewis
26. "Help Me Rhonda" by the Beach Boys
27. "Hey Jude" by the Beatles
28. "Hotel California" by the Eagles
29. "I Love this Bar" by Toby Keith
30. "I Will Survive" by Gloria Gaynor
31. "I'm a Believer" by the Monkees
32. "Imagine" by John Lennon
33. "Jack and Diane" by John Mellencamp
34. "The Joker" by Steve Miller
35. "King of the Road" by Roger Miller
36. "Let It Be" by the Beatles

37. "Living on a Prayer" by Bon Jovi
38. "Me and Bobbie McGee" by Janis Joplin
39. "My Girl" by the Temptations
40. "My Way" by Frank Sinatra
41. "Old Time Rock and Roll" by Bob Seger
42. "Proud Mary" by CCR/Tina Turner
43. "Red, Red Wine" by UB40
44. "Ring of Fire" by Johnny Cash
45. "Rocket Man" by Elton John
46. "Sweet Home Alabama" by Lynyrd Skynyrd
47. "Take Me Home Country Roads" by John Denver
48. "Under the Boardwalk" by the Drifters
49. "You've Lost That Loving Feeling" by the Righteous Brothers
50. "Your Song" by Elton John

Remember, think of these 50 titles as songs you *must* know, and get to work learning them. Make sure they are on any song list you provide an agent or booking contact. For an expanded list of several hundred songs you *should* know, see Appendix 3.

You may notice there are only four songs on the above list associated with female singers and none of them are in the Big-10. That's just the reality of the gig, and I'm not going to water it down to appear politically correct. Fortunately, I'm seeing increased numbers of successful female PBEs, and I think that's having a positive effect. Guests are requesting more songs from women artists at my shows, and I'm adding them to my repertoire all the time. I hope that in the future the must-know piano bar songs will be more gender balanced, but we're not there yet.

As for letting guests know what songs you can play, it is common to provide copies of a printed list that can be set around the bar and at tables. Some cruise lines provide their own "pre-approved" list, so you might need to ask your supervisor for permission to pass out your own. To help gain approval, you'd be wise to omit songs with adult content. Some PBEs put out binders with lists of every song they know. Others present a "favorites" list with one to two hundred songs. I prefer the latter and typically avoid listing most of the Big-10 because they will be requested no matter what, so I might as well get some other worthy songs on the short list. Whatever quantity you decide on, make your lists moisture resistant because it's inevitable drinks will get spilled and you need them to last for weeks or months. And remember that the font size of your list needs to be large enough for guests to read in a dimly lit lounge after they've had a couple drinks.

Your Music Gear

Guitarists, bassists, and horn players all carry their axes in a gig bag; even drummers usually carry their own sticks and cymbals. Fortunately, a PBE doesn't need to bring their own piano on a cruise ship, but that doesn't mean you won't have a gig bag full of important tools of the trade. Get yourself a sturdy shoulder bag with lots of pockets and fill it with the following "must have" items:

Tablet: having a tablet has quickly become the most important tool a PBE must own. In my earliest performance days I would travel with a large crate full of sheet music and fake books in order to meet guest requests. By the time I was able to dig up the desired song among the thousands of pages, it was very likely the guest had lost interest. Then another request would arrive and cause a repeat of the entire timely process. All of that has been solved by digital tablets capable of holding thousands of searchable files in the space of a narrow notebook. Some PBEs insist on only performing what they memorize so they can better engage the crowd. This is admirable, but I prefer to have the potential to play thousands of requests even if it means I'm reading from a screen. I think piano bar guests are far more pleased that I can say "yes" to their request than whether or not I have it memorized. The most popular songs should be memorized, but for all the rest, the tablet is the way to go. There are several song-organizing apps available, but I won't mention them by name because they could be gone or unsupported by the time you read this. Generally, how they work is that you load in PDF files (although other file types are accepted) and use the app to organize them by title, artist, keyword, or other possibilities. You can also create set lists, special "books" or collections, and back everything up to a computer or send it to other devices. My iPad sits on the piano music stand (set to the lowest possible slant to avoid it being a visual obstacle) where I am able to quickly call up whatever song I need. The apps have the ability to pull files from the internet, but don't count on using that feature in real-time on a ship. It doesn't take long to get quite adept at skimming the screen for lyrics and chords while mostly keeping your eyes up and engaging the audience.

Microphone: cruise ships will provide you a microphone, but bring your own to ensure quality and hygiene. To cut down on germs, don't share your mic, and use the ship's mic for guest singers. Take your mic with you at the end of each night. If you don't have your own yet, the industry standard vocal microphone used around the world for live performance is the Shure 58. You shouldn't worry about bringing a cable.

Piano key: this doesn't apply to digital pianos, but acoustic pianos might have locks to keep guests from playing them during the day so be sure to bring your own key. There should always be a key available on the ship, but it's amazing how often it gets lost. These are standard-sized keys across brand names and readily available on the internet. Mine has proven useful several times.

Tuning wrench: this only applies to acoustic pianos, but be prepared to tune a string now and then. If one gets knocked out of tune (rolling ships are hard on pianos) it could be weeks before a technician is scheduled for a visit so a temporary effort on your part might be needed.

Marketing material: you will probably be allowed to have a small sign on the piano listing your name and social media information. Do not include a phone number or home address because you don't want guests stalking you after their cruise is over. Guests following your fan page is great, but endlessly texting you or showing up at your house is not a good thing.

Consider the following items to be optional for your gig bag but still highly recommended:

Props: this might include things like silly sunglasses, kazoos, or feather boas. One of my props is a sparkly scarf that I use for certain Neil Diamond songs. There is much more discussion about using stage props in Chapter 3.

Merchandise for sale: selling CDs or download cards to guests is an excellent way to generate increased income and grow your fan base. Some PBEs even sell t-shirts or bumper stickers with their names and a catch phrase (I sell books). You will probably need to get the items pre-approved by your cruise line. One cruise line I worked for only allowed items to be sold through the gift shop and they took a percentage. Other cruise lines let you sell for cash in the piano bar and you keep it all. I've seen the more popular PBEs sell merchandise through their websites as well so they can continue to generate income even when they aren't on a ship.

Harmonica for "Piano Man:" it is not necessary to play the harmonica during the intro to "Piano Man," but guests absolutely love it if you do. I had never played harmonica in my life but was able to teach myself the intro in about 15 minutes, and you can too. I hold the harmonica in one hand while playing chords with the other. When purchasing the harmonica, make sure you get one in the right key for you. Billy Joel recorded his version in C but these days performs it in Bb (as do I).

Foot tambourine: I don't know how I ever got by without one of these. They are found online and have an elastic band that goes over your left shoe. By tapping your foot (something you probably already do) you keep the beat going and encourage guests to clap along. It's also a conversation starter because people wonder where the sound is coming from.

Anything else to get you through the performance: this may include aspirin, tissues, makeup, lip balm, tea, protein bar, breath mints, manicuring scissors for a torn fingernail, etc.

Social Media

If you work any length at all as a PBE, you should establish related social media accounts because guests will be thrilled to have a connection to the great time they had with you. If possible, the account names should have something to do with you as a performer and be easy to remember. Mine is "Piano Dude Gregg."

Some cruise lines even require you to sign a social media policy stating that you direct all guests to fan-based pages rather than a personal page. That's not bad advice. Giving guests too much access to your personal life online is asking for all sorts of stalking problems. I've had a couple of creepy situations, and PBEs I know have come to deeply regret getting too familiar with guests they met on a ship. It's common among crew to refer to passengers as "cones" because whenever you're in a hurry to get across the ship you can bet the corridors will be blocked by hundreds of slow moving guests that seem to sit there like traffic cones. You will meet some absolutely wonderful people from all over the world working as a PBE, and I fully encourage you to get to know them, but when the cruise is over, cones are cones. Let them follow your fan page and "like" your photos now and then, but the nature of the job is to love them madly for a cruise and then let them go. If guests find your personal pages and request to "friend" you, I suggest you try to let them know about your fan pages or simply ignore them.

You'll find guests from past cruises will gladly respond to your posts and let you know they still think about cruising with you. And guests booked on future cruises will look you up and let you know when they will join you. It's amazing how serious some people take the piano bar experience. For them, the piano bar is the most important aspect of their cruise entertainment and they will seek out information on you before they sail. There are social-media pages and websites dedicated to fans of cruise ship piano bars where they rate PBEs and ask if anyone has heard about a new name on the schedule. Having your own PBE-related social media presence (with video links) will give all your fans—past, present, and future—an easy way to see what you're up to without getting too personal.

Making Your Demo Package

Once upon a time, cruise ship musicians created a demo package that was literally sent in the mail as a package. It's all done digitally now, and the process is much more efficient. There is no "industry template" for documents or exactly what goes into a PBE demo package, but there is enough agreement that I can tell you what main components you will need to prepare before you're ready to solicit a gig.

Video: the most important item for your demo package is without a doubt a performance video. This is where you should put most your effort. Video shot from a phone is likely sufficient, but make sure you are the primary focus, the lighting is good, and the sound is clearly audible. Don't include full versions of songs. A verse and chorus is enough, then segue to the next title. Include your name in the video but not contact info (agents won't want clients contacting you directly). Use a variety of keys and piano accompaniment styles. An acoustic or digital piano is acceptable, but make sure you are performing without drum machines or backing tracks so it's obvious you can perform as a solo pianist. You might make your first video in your living room, but it is much better if you're in front of a crowd.

Protip: go to a local piano bar and tip the performer(s) $20 to play a couple songs while a friend records video. Encourage the crowd to clap or sing along. Do that a few times at different venues wearing different clothes, and it will look like you are a gigging machine. Collect all your videos together in editing software and cut it down to the best moments. The total length shouldn't be much more than 10-12 minutes. Upload the finished product to YouTube where it will be viewable by booking agents. In the description area for the video, list the song titles and starting times so viewers can skip ahead with ease. As for what songs you should include, there's no definitive answer because different cruise lines focus on different age demographics, but the following breakdown is likely to cover all the bases just fine:

1. **Four Sing-Alongs:** songs from the Big-10 like "Brown-eyed Girl," "Piano Man," "Joy to the World," "Sweet Caroline," "New York, New York" and "Friends in Low Places"
2. **Four Hi-Energy Pop/Rock:** songs like "Pour Some Sugar on Me," "Living on a Prayer," "Don't Stop Believing," and "Uptown Funk"
3. **Two Contemporary R&B:** popular songs from artists like Bruno Mars, Rihanna, or John Legend
4. **Two Modern Country:** popular songs from artists like George Strait, Carrie Underwood, Dierks Bentley, or Toby Keith
5. **One Island-Style:** songs like "Margaritaville," "Red, Red Wine," or "Three Little Birds"
6. **One Vocal Standard:** a classic like "Fly Me to the Moon," "My Way," or "Can't Help Falling in Love"

Photos: you can probably get by without a professional studio portrait at first, but try to gather some photos of you in performance mode or at least sitting at the piano. You want to look "in character" as if you already work as a PBE. During the agency application process, you'll likely be asked to upload a photo or two. Once you are working on a ship, you can probably get free photos taken by the staff photographers.

Résumé: agencies usually want a brief biography listing your previous performing experience and education. There is zero chance they will verify any of the information you provide. They just need something to pass on to cruise lines. You could use any standard template in Microsoft Word to create your document. Keep it simple without any prose. You're providing facts, not conversation or explanations.

Song List: include all the 50 songs from above and start adding songs from the expanded list in Appendix 3. I like to organize my list by decade or genre, but there's no standard. It isn't unusual to include songs on your list that you intend to learn by the time you get your first gig. In other words, you wouldn't be the first to "pad" your list, but don't go overboard.

While the photo, résumé, and song list are necessary, it's the video that will make things happen for you. A beautiful headshot with perfect lighting and makeup will not compensate for a video that doesn't highlight your musical strengths. It is not acceptable to include a note with your video saying, "Please ignore the cracked note in the verse, bad intonation on the chorus, and shaky piano playing; I was having a bad day and am usually much better." Toss that video out and make a new one that struts your stuff. It doesn't need to be musically flawless, but it should express professionalism and confidence so the viewer doesn't think it's your first rodeo (even if it is). You'll be better off taking the extra time to get it right than rushing ahead and botching your first impression.

Get Your Passport

While you are piecing together all the elements of your PBE starter kit and shoring up your musical skills, it could be months before you are ready to reach out about getting a contract offer. This is the perfect time to make sure your passport is current. The process of getting a passport is slow at best, so start early. I get emails every month for last-minute PBE offers all over the world, and only those with a passport in their hands can apply. You might as well make sure to have that detail checked off the list.

The tablet is a "must have"
(photo by Roy Mezzapelle)

CHAPTER 2: GETTING YOUR FIRST GIG

You're making some progress now. You've come to understand the true job description of the piano bar entertainer, assessed your strengths and weaknesses as a singer and pianist, assembled the items for your gig bag, have learned many or all of the 50 most important songs, created social media pages, got your passport updated, and put together a demo package with an excellent video. I'd say it's time to reach out about booking your first PBE gig. Congratulations on getting this far!

Finding and Contacting Agents

Most cruise ship lines need so many musicians and entertainers (singers, dancers, magicians, jugglers, disc jockeys, comedians, etc.) that they only accept applications submitted through a booking agency they already have a relationship with. About the only cruise line you can book directly with is Carnival, so they will be discussed separately. First, let's talk about how things work with booking agents.

In plenty of old movies that feature a lead character who is an entertainer, there is often an agent who works tirelessly to find his client work and doubles as his confidante, manager, and best buddy. Yeah, that's not how it works anymore. Perhaps there was a time when the agent worked as a pseudo employee of the entertainer, but now it often feels the other way around. The agent has most of the power, and the entertainer just hopes to stay in good graces.

Finding an agency that books cruise line entertainers is not hard. They want to be found and probably already show up in advertisements on your social media feeds. In addition, you likely have a friend or two with previous cruise ship experience who can refer you. If not, an internet search will get you a list of potential contacts. I've also included a short list in Appendix 1. Look through the websites for each and read what they have to offer. Do they seem currently active or is the site dated? Are they run by former cruise ship musicians who have real-world experience? Is the agency a large business or one person (they both have advantages)?

Here's a step-by-step breakdown of how the relationship progresses between an agent and a PBE.

The Process of Working with an Agent

1. You do the research and find an agency with a good reputation that you feel comfortable working with. Never pay a fee up front! Reputable agencies don't work that way. They will charge a fee based on a percentage of your salary that comes later. The agency gets paid when you get paid. Currently, the percentage agencies take is at least 10% but shouldn't be over 15%.

2. You make first contact, likely as an email or submission form on a website, in which you will give them a link to your demo video.

3. Hopefully, they quickly respond and request more information from you. This might include a phone call. They will have already watched your video link and give you some feedback.

4. If the video is sufficient, they will probably invite you to fill out a more complete application and accept you onto their roster of piano bar entertainers. If they see a problem with the video, but are confident in your potential, they will ask if you can get some other video for them to make up the deficiency (this was my situation for my first booking). Or, if they don't think they can use you, they might invite you to contact them again at a later time. Don't assume they are making a negative judgement about your skills; it's possible they just aren't booking PBEs at the moment. Start over with another agency. If two or three agencies all pass, your materials need to be stronger. Keep practicing, make a new video, and try again later.

5. Assuming you pass the video "audition" and are now on the agency's roster, there's not much you can do until the next step. It is assumed that you are only working with the one agency and not several at the same time. Agencies don't want to put in the time booking you only to find you already got the same booking through someone else.

6. You will receive a "request to submit." This might take days or a couple months. A "request to submit" means the agency has a lead on a PBE opening and wants to submit your package for the job but wants to make sure you are available before doing so. They will give you the dates and potential money to be made and you let them know if they should proceed. I encourage you to always say yes. You can change your mind later, but you want to try and get the real offer with the full details.

7. You get a real offer! Your video impresses the right people at a cruise line and they want you as their PBE. Congratulations! The next steps depend on the agency you're working with. My first contract offer was with a large agency that had a contract agreement with the cruise line so they assisted me through much of the process of getting hired and acted as a conduit for all the communication. I was offered a post-commission salary, so I didn't actually know what the agency commission was. The next agency I worked with was a one-man shop, and once I received the contract offer he turned me over to the cruise line's application process and only got involved if there was a problem. That situation led to two contracts being required: one with the cruise line stating the full salary for the position, and another with the agency stating the commission I would pay them once the salary started. In that case, I knew exactly what the commission was because I wrote the check. The second offer had a higher gross salary, but after disbursing the commission from my own pocket, both jobs ended up paying about the same.

8. From this point you will hear from the agent whenever there are more details about the job, like your medical exam and travel. The smoother things are going, the less you will hear from them. This would be a good time to ask if the cruise line has a song list that will be available to guests in the piano bar and how you can get a copy.

9. Looking ahead, you can reach out to the agency during your contract if you'd like them to work on getting you another gig as soon as possible. Once you've gotten your first contract done, it's much easier finding more work because cruise lines prefer a PBE with experience. You might also hear from your agency if the cruise

line wants to extend your contract beyond the original agreement. Requests like that are common.

10. When you get a second offer, the process starts over again but will be much simpler if it's with the same cruise line. If it's with a new line, they will almost certainly require a new medical exam, even if they are owned by the same company you already worked for.

11. Agencies also have a line placed somewhere in their contracts stating that once they get you a booking, you are not allowed to book yourself directly with that cruise line for 7 years! And this is renewable every time you accept a new contract, so essentially, once an agency has booked you with cruise line X, you will need to use that agency any time you ever work for X again.

What a Booking Agency Can Do for You

Booking agencies can: give you advice to improve your demo package; get you a job offer; act as a communication conduit between you and the cruise line; deliver the details of the gig to you; find answers to details you want to know more about; get your travel information; negotiate salary for you; help you on the ship if major details are far from what you agreed to; find a music store at one of your ports because you have a gear emergency; and help get your next contract.

What a Booking Agency Cannot Do for You

Booking agencies cannot: make you a better video; get overly specific answers about ship life (*i.e.*, "What brand of soy milk is available in the crew mess?"); help with basic complaints once on board about your cabin, internet quality, food, or access to the guest gym; respond to guests who complain about you; get you more pay once you've signed the contract; or keep you from being fired if you break a serious crew policy.

Problems with Booking Agents

By far, the biggest problem I have witnessed concerning booking agents is their willingness to place musicians in inappropriate jobs. They only get paid a commission once a musician is on a gig so, in their anxiousness, I think there are times booking agents look the other way when it comes to specific details. You might think you've asked all the right questions about song lists, tip jars, and cabin accommodations only to arrive at the gig and find nothing is as you were told by the agent. When you confront them, you will likely get nothing more than an apologetic email. You are already on the ship and they know you aren't likely to walk off the gig at that point. You're stuck making the best of a job that isn't quite what you were expecting.

Fortunately, as a PBE ready to sing and play highly interactive material for hours at a time, you will avoid the most common booking problem I see in piano bars. Usually what happens is a pianist who can barely sing and only knows a few dozen songs is booked on what they think is a background cocktail pianist gig only to be thrown into a lion's den of piano bar fans expecting all their favorite bawdy sing-alongs. Your best bet to avoid inappropriate bookings is to ask as many questions as possible and don't settle for answers like, "We'll look into that." Better yet, do some research and try to contact a PBE who had the gig before you so you'll learn what the job is really like.

Salary Negotiation

The previous point about not being able to book directly with a cruise line for seven years after using an agent is why there's a strong argument for booking directly on your own. The problem is, most cruise lines won't book you without an agency. It's a bit of a racket in which the agencies and cruise lines have decided they can both make more money in the long run if they keep the artists out of the process as much as possible. That said, using a booking agency is not inherently a bad deal. I've worked with multiple agencies and have found them to be professional and able to deliver what they promised. It's true that I wasn't keeping all the money the cruise line actually paid out for the position, but I was working a gig that I never would have been able to book myself anyway.

For your first contract offer, I suggest you take whatever salary is being paid unless it seems unusually low (refer to the Introduction for salary ranges). Let's face it, you need the experience. For future contracts you can negotiate salary upwards and simply tell your agent what the minimum is you will work for (after commission). At that point, the agent can decide to reduce their commission or try to get more salary from the cruise line. I've had both of those situations occur. It's a balancing act to be paid what you think you're worth but not price yourself higher than what the market will tolerate. Between my first and second contracts with the same cruise line I negotiated a 10% raise. I was offered an additional 20% to accept a third contract but passed because I had an even better offer elsewhere. The money for PBEs is out there if you keep looking.

Contacting Cruise Lines Direct

This could change, but at the moment the only major cruise line that allows musicians to book through an agency or direct is Carnival Cruise Lines. All you have to do is visit the website www.carnivalentertainment.com and follow the directions to apply as a piano bar entertainer. You will upload your demo materials and video link through their submission form. If they think your material is strong enough, they will invite you to "formally" audition and send you information about creating a new video for them with specific requirements. If you followed my video recommendations in Chapter 1 you'll be nearly ready to go. You will have to edit your video slightly to include a personal statement explaining why you'd be a good fit for Carnival. This is really just a way for them to make sure that as a PBE you have good communication skills in English. It's not so important what you say as how you say it. Keep it short, clear, and show a little personality. Consider making your statement in a performance-like setting, or, if you live near a terminal, position yourself with a cruise ship in the background. I actually created my statement while on a competitor's cruise ship and said I was ready to "trade up."

You can expect to hear a response from Carnival within a couple weeks, at which point you are hopefully added to their PBE roster. They state that a first offer can take up to two months, but they gave me one in under three weeks. It could be a contract that doesn't start for a couple months or an emergency replacement that starts in two days. Be prepared for anything and try to say "yes" to whatever comes your way. After receiving a positive evaluation at the end of your first contract, you will be given access to an online system that allows you to request future contracts. Keep in mind that even though Carnival Corporation owns several other cruise lines, you would only be working on ships specifically in the Carnival branded line known as CCL. To work for one of their other cruise lines in the corporation like Holland-America, P & O, Costa, or Princess, you would have to go through an agency.

At the moment, Carnival (CCL) offers a competitive salary and allows a tip jar so it is possible to considerably increase your weekly take. You may ask, "Why would I ever use an agency if I can book direct with Carnival?" Two reasons come to mind. The piano bars on Carnival ships are known for exceptionally high energy and crowds that want to be constantly entertained. If your style as a PBE is subtler, Carnival isn't for you. Secondly, Carnival ships primarily serve the Caribbean so if you'd like more options around the world, you'll want to pursue other cruise lines.

All About Your Medical Exam

During the time between accepting a contract and leaving for the ship is when you will need to complete and pass a Pre-Employment Medical Exam or PEME. Passing your exam can be time consuming no matter how healthy you are, so take the task very seriously and start the process as soon as possible. The cruise line (possibly through your booking agent) will send you the information on where to go and what forms you will need.

Why is getting an approved PEME difficult? There are many reasons, but they all lead back to the fact that cruise lines offer employees free health care while you are on their ships. This is a wonderful perk of employment. You can see a doctor or nurse any day of the week and not be charged for resulting treatment and medication. If you need outside medical care, the ship's medical office will schedule you an appointment at one of the ports and the expenses are taken care of for you. But because cruise lines offer free health care, they do everything they can to hire only healthy people who won't likely need healthcare. This means they will be quite strict when reviewing your exam results and might balk at any abnormality. And medical staff have veto power over hiring any new employee no matter how much the entertainment department wants you.

Unfortunately, there is no industry standard as to what qualifies as healthy. One PBE I know had his PEME denied because he listed a prescription drug that his previous cruise line had no problem with. One cruise line adheres to weight limits while others go by Body Mass Index numbers. One cruise line I worked for insisted I sign a waiver stating they would hire me but not supply any health care related to one of my test results. Two years later (a PEME needs to be renewed every two years) they stopped accepting waivers and wouldn't approve me until my condition was reversed. I did the work, re-tested a month later and passed, but it was a stressful ordeal.

Another hindrance to completing your exam can be the location. Sometimes I was able to use clinics in my home area, including my own doctor. But my first contract was with a small cruise line, and the nearest facility they insisted I use was a six-hour drive that nearly kept me from accepting the position.

A third issue with the PEME is the cost. Depending on the cruise line, you will cover most or all of the exams fees. I have paid as little as $300 and as much as $550. The costs vary depending on where you have the exam, if you need vaccines, and if you are over 50 (older crew need more tests). Even though the PEME is good for two years, you will likely have to renew it before the expiration date because when you join a ship the PEME must be good for the entire length of your contract. This means your expense is spread out over less time than the cruise lines would have you believe. In reality you will actually be paying $300-$550 about every 20-22 months for your "free" healthcare.

Lastly, the same PEME is not accepted across all cruise lines. If you want to work for different companies, you will go through the entire medical exam process all over again and pay a new round of fees. This can get expensive. And keep in mind that if you are ever denied, you have to absorb the cost of the exam without ever receiving any salary from that company.

Next to preparing a great video of your performance skills, getting through the medical approval is the most important step for becoming a PBE. Your best path forward is to stay healthy, answer "no" to as many questions as possible on the PEME, and start the process early so you have time to deal with any obstacles that come your way.

Once you receive your approved PEME, treat it like a precious family heirloom. You must bring the ORIGINAL signed document with you to the ship. Never pack it with your checked luggage that might get lost. Keep it with you in a carry-on bag. On the ship you will hand it over to the medical staff for their review. When they return the document to you, do not leave their sight until you look through it to make sure nothing is missing. The three most important items to your PBE cruise ship career are your tablet, passport, and PEME. You could lose everything else, but with those three things you could still get on the ship and start selling that alcohol!

If you know you have a medical condition or history that would preclude you from passing a PEME, all hope of being a PBE is not lost. You may be able to be hired as a short-term replacement when last-minute gaps in calendars open up. If you are hired for only 1-3 weeks, you are considered "fly-on" entertainment as opposed to regular crew who need a PEME. It's not ideal, but at least you can still get a taste for being a PBE.

How to Pack Your Bags

Packing for months at a time might be a new experience for you. The tendency is to overpack and bring countless items you don't need. Not only is it a burden to haul all that extra content, it can also be expensive if you are charged over-the-weight-limit fees by the airlines. The cruise line you work for will usually only reimburse you for standard fees on up to two checked bags. Be sure to save receipts for the bag fees you pay or you won't get the money back.

I have learned how to pack everything I need in one checked bag and two carry-on bags, but I realize that not all of you can live as Spartan as I do, so you might need two checked bags. Just keep in mind that you're the one who will have to maneuver those bags through airports, on and off shuttle buses, and up and down gangways that sometimes get very lengthy and steep. Hard-shell luggage seems to be the most common among crew members who've been at it for a while. I've yet to have my baggage lost or damaged, but it happens often enough to be a concern. As a precaution, I pack everything I need to work as a performer in my carry-on bags. This includes all my "gig bag" items and important documents (letter of employment, hotel and travel information, passport, and medical approval). While on the plane I wear clothes that could potentially work on stage. For me this includes: black jeans, black long-sleeved shirt, and my stage hat. In the worst-case scenario of my checked bags being sent to the other side of the world, I know I have the ability to get on the ship and put on a show.

For a specific list of everything I bring with me on a contract and what bag it goes in, see Appendix 2.

Travel and Arriving at Your Ship

On your travel day, I suggest you put at least $100 cash in your pocket for food, tips, ground transportation if needed, and purchasing internet when you get to the ship. If your gig doesn't allow a tip jar, you'll want to bring more cash to cover expenses until your first payday.

Hopefully, your flights go smoothly and you arrive at your destination airport with all your luggage. At this point, you will work your way to ground transportation and be taken to the hotel arranged for you by the cruise line (if you arrive on the sailing date, you will be sent straight to the ship). Once at the hotel, you will show them your letter of employment and they will assign you a room for the night that should include meal vouchers for dinner and breakfast. If you encounter any problems, call your agent or reach out to the cruise line's 24-hour travel assistance center that you should have been given contact information for. Stay calm and let people who deal with travel issues all day long come up with a solution. I've had to make calls for help from a couple hotel lobbies, and it got resolved before I hung up.

The hotel will likely have a notebook or notice board with cruise ship information you'll want to consult. Find your name and double check you are on the list for the ship you are expecting. There will also be information about what time you need to meet in the morning to take the crew shuttle to the port. It won't take you long to learn that crew members have a certain look—young and international—so when in doubt, look for your fellow crew to tell you what's going on.

Arriving at the ship, you'll wait in a series of lines where you will likely show various forms of ID until you are finally allowed onboard. The first stop is usually a crew office where they begin processing you as a joining crew member. Just go with the flow; these people perform this job every week and generally know what they are doing. Before you leave the office, you'll be given your cabin assignment and a door key/card, as well as information about what you'll need to do the rest of your first day. Take all this info to your cabin and relax a few minutes as you recover from information overload.

If you're brand new to ships, your Music Director should reach out to see how you are doing. If not, take a little time and walk around the ship to get oriented. It will take several days to get used to the layout of starboard, port, forward, mid, and aft, but you'll soon learn it all makes sense. Find your way to the piano bar and check out the environment. Try out the piano (you might need your key to unlock the lid), explore the lights and sound equipment a little, and take inventory of supplies like request slips and song lists. Before you start your first show later that night, a technician should meet with you to do a sound check, set the lights, and show you the basics of how to make changes. For the most part, the piano bar is a self-contained room where you take care of your own sound/lights after the first night unless there is a problem.

Protip: take a picture of the mixing board when things sound good so you can always get everything back to that point when needed. Piano bars are often used during the day for other events, and it's amazing how often the mixing board gets completely changed between PBE performances.

There will almost certainly be an orientation the first afternoon for new "sign-ons" where you will get initial information about safety and emergency evacuation. You will probably be assigned your "emergency duty" that designates what you will do if the crew is called to alert. Before the ship sails, there will be a safety briefing for guests and you will report to your emergency station to assist with guests. Of course, on your first day you won't know enough to be of much help, so just try not to be too much in the way. After a few weeks, you'll be up to speed and can answer all the usual questions guests ask (the most common are about getting food, locating smoking areas, and when their cabin will be ready).

After the sail away, you'll have time for dinner and can get a good taste of what the crew dining experience is all about. Then it's back to your cabin to get cleaned up and ready for your first big show. Get dressed in your stage clothes, strap on your gig bag, check yourself in the mirror to make sure your wearing a name tag, and head for the piano bar because it's business time baby!

CHAPTER 3: PLAYING YOUR GIG

You jumped through all the hoops to prepare for and secure your first gig, you survived your travel day and overwhelming first day on a ship, and made it to the piano bar for your first show! This is what you've been waiting for and easily the best part of your job as a PBE. Traveling to far off ports and meeting interesting people is wonderful, but playing your gig is why you're really a musician in the first place. Let's break down exactly what your performance should look like so that at the end of the night you can confidently say, "Nailed it."

Your Persona and Presentation Are More Important Than the Music

The above statement is tough for many musicians to accept. Get over it. I have sat through meetings of the entertainment department on cruise ships where management said loud and clear that they consider artistic craft to be only 15% of what they want us to focus on. The remaining 85% should be based on image and engagement with the guests to make personal connections. I really didn't like hearing that my decades spent being the best musician possible was only valued at 15%. But not only did I get over it, I learned how to exploit it in ways that don't take much effort and still allowed me self-respect as a musician. Here's how:

Memorize Guest Names: you can do this through personal conversations or by looking at request slips that include names. I like to politely ask guests around the piano for their names. Then I ask where they're from and if their having a good time so far. While they are talking I am actually barely listening. Instead, I'm repeating their names over and over in my mind while looking at their faces to make the association. By the time they are done talking, I've got their names memorized, and the next night when they walk through the doors I call out, "Hey Bob and Susan, great to see you!" I've just made their night. If people leave the bar before I get their names I can also ask the bartender to check receipts for the information.

Learning Songs for Guests: if guests make requests for a song you think would be a good addition to your repertoire, tell them, "Give me a couple days, and I'll see what I can do." When they come back, make an announcement that you've learned the song just for them before you perform it. You want everyone in the room to know you made the extra effort.

Protip: I've gone as far as to say I would learn a song I already know and play it a couple days later as if it was the first time. This is a great way to keep generating tips for songs already on your list. And the guests feel special so no harm done. See Appendix 5 for tips on the most efficient way to learn songs.

Smile, Though Your Heart Is Aching: that's a line from an old song by Charlie Chaplin and holds very true for PBEs. I learned a valuable lesson by watching video of myself years ago playing at a gig where I know I had a great time. But from the video you'd think I was miserable. I have since trained myself to keep smiling all night long. At first, I had to consciously remind myself, "Smile Gregg.

Keep smiling." These days it's automatic, and I rarely think about it, but I get constant guest comments about what a nice smile I have and that I "always look so happy performing." It's true that I'm usually in a good mood on stage, but even if I'm not, I'm still smiling. Guests have been saving all year for their exotic cruise experience, and I'm there to help them have a great time, not wondering if I'm bored or angry.

Keep Your Eyes Up: making eye contact with guests is one of the easiest things you can do to make a lasting impression. I use a technique I call "Scan and Smile." I start on my left and look at the first guest in the eyes until they look back. I maintain the connection long enough that they know I really am looking at them and not just glancing that direction. Then I simply smile. That one act has made the biggest impact on my performance style. I've learned that there are thousands of lonely people out there, sometimes even those sitting right next to a spouse, who just want to be acknowledged. The person I'm looking at usually smiles back, but if not, I don't worry about it. Then I move my gaze to the right and repeat the process. By the time I get all the way to my right I've made connections with everyone in the room. I do this several times a night because new people come and go. After a few nights of a week-long cruise, I've got a piano bar full of guests who all feel we have a special connection simply because I acknowledged them several times with a smile. By the end of a cruise, I've given some guests more personal attention than they've had in years! An added bonus is that keeping your eyes off your hands increases your skill as a pianist, but that's for your own satisfaction as a musician. Guests just like that you're looking at them.

Reading the Room: as you scan the room night after night you'll start to notice certain types of crowds. Most the guests are just pleasant people ready to have a nice time being entertained. That is the main group you should direct your energy towards. However, there are a few sub-sets some guests fall into I think are worth mentioning:

1. **Looky-Loo's:** these folks usually show up early in your set, sit as far away as possible, don't want to interact or sing along yet send up piles of requests for Big-10 songs, and as soon as some other show starts in another area they leave without tipping. There's really nothing you can do with this crowd to change their behavior other than be polite and wait them out. Don't burn through your A-list songs for this group. Say, "Here's one you requested," and then play a song of your own choosing. The looky-loo crowd will think you're playing requests but just haven't gotten to theirs yet.
2. **Tip Jumpers:** when I first started working cruise ships, I often wondered why I saw large numbers of people in the piano bar on the last night of the cruise whom I hadn't seen before. They didn't seem interested in the music, but they sat there stoically having a couple drinks. A veteran bartender explained to me they were tip jumpers. These are guests who spent all week receiving quality drink service in another lounge, and then on the last night when it is customary to hand over a large tip for the week's effort, they "jump" to a different lounge to get their buzz on but aren't expected to tip much because they are new to that room. Be polite, but basically ignore them or their requests. (Side note: as a PBE you get paid a decent salary by American standards. The bulk of your crew mates, however, make literally a few dollars a day in salary; making tips their true source of income. This is the business model for all cruise lines and why none of them are based in America where

there are minimum-wage laws. Unfortunately, tip jumpers have no idea how much damage they do to the people who ensured great service throughout the cruise.)
3. **Piano Bar-barians:** these are self-proclaimed lovers of all things piano bar and are usually a lot of fun. These are the guests who educate others how to have fun in a piano bar. They know they are supposed to tip for requests, like to interact, and can help raise the energy of the entire room. They can also act entitled and try to dictate the direction of your show so don't let them push you around. They are on your turf, not the other way around. If a noisy guy grumbles ten minutes into your first set that you better start playing his favorite dirty songs or he's leaving, let him leave. He'll be back eventually and will know who's in charge.

Developing a Style of Presentation

I'm sure there have been many PBEs in the past who insisted on being appreciated only for their musical skills and refused to "sell out" to being an entertainer. I'm also sure they are all working in jobs outside of entertainment these days. If you have amazing songs you've written and want to pursue a career as a solo artist clear of mainstream influence, I hope you reach your dream, but that's not what a PBE is, so don't confuse the two. Do not become a PBE hoping to change the job description. You'll only end up frustrated and ultimately unemployed after fighting against the system for a couple years. Your job is not to educate guests on what your idea of good music is, it's to play songs everybody already loves and SELL ALCOHOL.

To really excel as a PBE, you need to develop a style of presentation that guests are drawn to and will remember. Be creative and try to incorporate your own personality into the mix. You don't need to be fake, but you might have to bring out aspects of your personality that you don't always show. Guests want to think they are seeing a character based on the real you. Here are some ideas to make that happen:

Clothes: PBEs are fortunate in that we don't have an official uniform to wear on ship like many other crew members. You get to establish your own uniform. Will it be classy? Western? Urban? Retro-hippy? Classic rockstar? I've seen some successful PBEs go with jeans and a tank-top, but I think you should let people know that when you walk through the doors there is no mistaking you as the entertainer. You want them to remember you.

Hats/Glasses/Jewelry: These items can change from night to night or even song to song and help engage the guests. For example, I have one pair of sunglasses for when I play songs by Elton John and another pair for disco songs. I've seen a PBE who puts on a straw sun-hat only when he plays Jimmy Buffett. If your ship has nights for Mardi Gras or a glow party, play along and wear a related necklace for the evening.

Stage Props and Toys for Guests: some ships may already have a supply of props/toys for you to give guests, but you might consider bringing your own; these include things like feather boas, inflatable air-guitars, small tambourines, and shakers.

Comedy Bits: adding comedy to your show will take a lot of effort and may even introduce an element of risk because not everyone interprets humor the same way. I suggest taking note of when you or a guest naturally say something that gets a big laugh. At the end of the night, write down what was said and use it on a future cruise.

I have a bit where I learn the name of the loudest "look at me" guy in the room and in the middle of a song I stop playing and say, "Hey Bob, tell us a dirty joke." Of course, Bob (or whoever) loves the attention and launches into a joke. If it's funny, I'm the clever guy who allowed it to be told. If it bombs, it's his fault, and I make fun of it the rest of the night. The bit works either way. Some PBEs are excellent at inviting guests to the stage area and getting them involved in a comedy bit, but this can get awkward if you're not careful. I once had an inebriated guest fall backwards off the stage and hit her head, creating an embarrassing and possibly dangerous situation. To get more ideas on comedy bits, visit dueling piano bars and watch how they get the crowd involved for birthdays and anniversaries. There's no law against taking notes and borrowing from others with more experience, although be cool about it and leave a large tip before you leave.

Toasts: I've known PBEs who run their entire evening on a rotation of Toasts, Roasts, and Sing-Alongs. The roast is an acknowledgement of a special occasion guests are celebrating like a birthday or anniversary. The sing-along is one from the top-50 list in Chapter 1. And toasts are spoken tributes, usually comedic, meant to get everyone drinking. Years ago, I did an internet search for "toasts" and saved several to my iPad. Eventually, I memorized some of the best ones. I also learned to ask if any guests have a toast they'd like to share. Like the "look at me" guy mentioned above, there's always someone willing to speak up.

Encouraging Requests and Tips

Encouraging guests to tip you without blatantly begging is an artform. I know this subject is something that bothers guests because I have had several tell me, "I hate it when the pianist tells me he won't play any request without getting money." I think the problem has grown from the popularity of dueling piano bars where the entire performance is tip-driven. Cruise lines have decided they want the energy of dueling piano bars on their ships and have made efforts to recruit those entertainers. The problem is, "duelers" bring their assertive tip solicitations with them and cruise guests complain because they aren't used to it.

The challenge becomes, how do you get people to tip you without appearing to be a mooch? Not to mention the fact that even if a cruise line allows you a tip jar, they probably have a policy that says you are not allowed to specifically ask for tips. Here are some proven tactics to maneuver around such a conundrum:

1. Put some "starter" money in the tip jar so that people can see that tips are both allowed and encouraged.

Protip: I always start with $20 made up of mixed bills in the bowl so I know how much I actually made at the end of the night. This can also serve as change if a guest wants to break a $20 in order to tip me smaller amounts.

2. Early in the show when several requests arrive at the piano, I hold up the one with money so everyone can see and say, "For no particular reason, I think I'll play this one first." I usually get a laugh and it lets people know that money gets their song played sooner.

3. Sometimes I'll say, "This next request comes with an endorsement from Abraham Lincoln and Abe always gets what he wants."

4. If a request slip comes with money and includes the city a guest is from, I'll hold it up high and say, "This is a guest from [insert city] where they clearly know how to get things done!"

5. There's also a long-standing tradition that PBEs make a distinction between "suggestions" (no tip) and "requests" (with tip) and if you use those terms guests start to pick up on it and play along. If I announce, "I put suggestions on the left side of the piano but requests go on the right side," it doesn't take long for guests to figure out what I'm doing and start playing along.

6. Set a mini basketball hoop over the tip jar and you'll be surprised how competitive guests get trying to shoot their balled up money through the target. This encourages tipping without you having to say a word. The only downside is taking the time to flatten dozens of bills at the end of the night.

There are always going to be guests who stiff you. It's frustrating, but you have to deal with it. Sometimes they just aren't carrying cash and will catch up tipping you the next night. Sometimes they will offer to buy you a drink instead of giving you cash (this isn't an option for me because I don't drink alcohol or soda during my shows). Sometimes they are just cheap bastards who don't see anything wrong with expecting you to play all of their requests for free. Regardless, refrain from ever insulting someone for not tipping. You don't know their story. I have literally had some of my lowest and highest nights of tipping occur back to back during the same cruise and there's no predicting it. Just keep putting on a great show and over the long run it all evens out and you should make good money.

How to Say "No" to a Request

A common problem for new PBEs is never wanting to say to "no" to a guest request. But the most popular requests by far come from the Big-10 and if you play them all in the first half hour you've put yourself in a hole. The guests who arrive in the second half-hour will think they've arrived soon enough to hear those songs too. So the newbie, still not wanting to say no, plays them all again. Guess what will happen in second hour? The cycle repeats itself, but by now the guests who have been present all night are bored of hearing the same handful of titles for the third time. If the same thing happens the next night, those guests won't come back again.

This can be easily solved by learning how to say no with politeness and/or humor. Try these ideas:

1. When you get a request in the first few minutes for a Big-10 with a guest's name on it say, "It's piano bar law that whoever asks for [insert song title] first has to buy the house a round of drinks, so everybody let Brian from Orlando know what you want." This gets a laugh and stops others from sending up the same request for a while.

2. You can also try, "I got a few suggestions here for some awesome songs, and I promise I'll get to them eventually, but think of this as our first date and those are more like third-date songs."

3. Or, "I love the song you suggested, and I'll definitely play it later, but for now here's another one from the same artist I bet you know."

The caveat to all this is if a guest includes a large tip with their request. They get what they want when they want it. On the other hand, if a guest writes several songs on a request slip with no tip, just play one selection that makes the most sense at the moment and leave the rest for other guests who will tip. The thing to remember is that *you* run the show, not the guests. If the room is full of senior citizens and one Generation-X guy comes in shouting for Metallica, *do not* play it. Play to the entire room, not to one loud person who thinks they know what everyone should hear. Always remember, it's okay to say, "no." You might make that one person grumble, but everyone else in the room will know what's going on and appreciate that you're not allowing the show to be hijacked. The guests might try pushing you, but they actually don't want you to be a push-over.

Be careful about saying "no" to a request simply because you're bored playing that song. "Sweet Caroline" often falls into that category. Just the other night, I had already played the song twice that evening when a newly arrived guest asked for it again. She offered a $10 tip so I decided to grin my way through it for a third time. Afterwards, she whispered in my ear, "That made my night. The doctors tell me I have only a few months to live so I'm looking for every moment of fun I can get." Imagine what I would have taken away from her by pulling attitude and refusing to play her request?

The "Arc" of Your Show

Personally, I would never perform in a piano bar with a pre-determined set list because it completely undermines the concept of taking requests and playing to the room. But there is something to be said for considering the overall arc of energy the show takes. Think of your show like a good action movie that needs to develop dramatic energy over time, has a climactic moment, and a final scene to wrap up loose ends. If you have a subdued room early in the show, hitting them with "Pour Some Sugar on Me" is wasting an otherwise useful song. You'd be wiser to take it easy for a while and probe the crowd for what they seem interested in. Try some Motown, country, Jimmy Buffett, or John Legend until you get a reaction. As things get rolling you'll be up to the Def Leppard level in no time. After hitting the crowd with a series of sing-along show stoppers, start thinking about how you will wind up the set. Is it the kind of show that you want to end on a high note so that they stick around for more to come? If so, "Don't Stop Believing" or "Bohemian Rhapsody" is the way to go. Or are you finishing for the night and want to end with a pensive tone that says, "thank you for listening?" That situation calls for "Hallelujah," "What a Wonderful World," or "Can't Help Falling in Love."

An issue out of your control is exactly how long your sets are each night. I've worked for cruise lines that schedule only three 45-minute sets a night but with a long dinner break between two of them. Other cruise lines will have you start at 9 pm with no scheduled breaks until 1 a.m. In that case, you take only one or two (or zero) breaks depending on the ebb and flow of the crowd. For the longer shows, you may have several complete arcs throughout the evening. Stay flexible and keep scanning the room for feedback.

Adult Material

There is a small but exceptionally loud portion of piano bar guests who enjoy songs that are in the category of "late night" or "adult content." As you can guess, the subject matter of the lyrics is usually in the rated R or X arena. I provide a sample list of these songs in Appendix 3. I have worked for cruise lines that say, "Don't go there," others who say, "Go there if guests request it," and still others who say, "Go there all you want after a set time." For the latter, a notice is likely put in the daily schedule that specifically lists your later shows as "18 and over."

Even if a cruise line allows adult songs, the choice to do so is completely up to the PBE. I know PBEs who make it the centerpiece of most every evening and they have a deeply supportive fan base. I also know PBEs who don't play any adult songs at all and seem to do just fine. Personally, I fall into the category of "sometimes I will play a couple adult songs." This means I only "go there" if 1) someone is tipping me, 2) there are no kids in the room, and 3) the song is not derogatory towards a person or group. That last point can be subjective, but it's my show, so I get to decide. Songs that meet my threshold are usually more cheeky than trashy. This includes titles like "My Ding a Ling" or "Seven Drunken Nights." Other adult songs I might do include rated R words sung as a response by the audience rather than me, as happens in "Alice" and "Lucille." By the way, if you're wondering why there would ever be kids in a bar, just trust me on this, it happens all the time on a ship. Personally, I enjoy their presence and have found that by interacting with the kids and getting them to smile, the parents almost always tip me to show appreciation.

If your personality is in league with adult songs, then you will certainly find an audience, and there is plenty of potential material to be found on the internet. If, however, you'd rather veer away from such things, don't let a crowd bully you into playing songs you don't feel comfortable with. As I said before, it's your show and you can always say no. For every guest who grumbles about it, there are likely several more who support the decision you made.

Post-Performance Reflection

The bright lights have faded to blue, and the show in the piano bar has concluded. Hopefully a good time was had by all. Each night, you'll spend several minutes cleaning up your stage area, gathering your tips, and putting covers on the equipment, so this is when you should take a moment to reflect on your performance and identify what worked and what needs improvement. This may include songs that need more rehearsal, songs guests loved, songs guests ignored, requests you'll want to learn, and adjustments you'd like made to the sound or lighting. Feel good about making it through the night, and learn from both your successes and mistakes. Then get some rest because it all starts over in about 20 hours.

CHAPTER 4: KEEPING YOUR GIG

Your entertainment skills certainly play an important part in making your employer happy and keeping your gig, but it should not come at the expense of focusing on the bigger topic known simply as "ship life." Crew members often use the hashtag #shiplife in social media and it can be in reference to something positive or negative. Either way, anyone who has worked on a cruise ship reads the post, nods, and says, "Yup, I've been there." Keeping the gig you've worked so hard to acquire won't be possible unless you learn to navigate the main components of ship life so let's take the time to walk you through them.

Life on a Cruise Ship

Management Hierarchy: the most common chain of command above the PBE starts with the Music Director, also called the Music Manager. He or she performs in one of the musical acts and is who you will report to first for most issues. They provide you with a schedule and notices for trainings and anything you need to attend. Above the MD is the Entertainment Director who is in charge of all entertainers and overseeing the master schedule. You will interact with the ED on occasion but mostly with the MD. Usually, the Cruise Director is the face of the crew for the guests but answers to the ED and does not directly supervise any of the musicians. In an older system, still used by some cruise lines, the CD did both the work of guest-relations and the ED. Above the ED is the Hotel Director who manages all aspects of the hotel portion of the ship. The HD pops in for a departmental meeting now and then, but you might go weeks without seeing them. Above the HD (and everyone else) is the Captain whom except for a quick hello in a corridor, you will never likely interact with. One of the quickest ways to lose favor among your superiors is to circumvent chain of command. Whenever in doubt, start with your MD and then proceed upward as needed.

Trainings and Assessments: starting your first week on a ship you will be scheduled for several training sessions regarding safety, crew policies, vessel familiarization, environmental protection, and crowd management. No one enjoys these trainings, but no one gets out of them. Once the initial round of trainings is complete, you will only have to attend for renewals or new programs. Unfortunately, you'll likely have to sit through several of the same sessions every time you join a ship for a contract.

Crew Safety Drills: once a week crew have to participate in a safety drill. One or two cruise lines exempt PBEs from emergency duties, but with the others you will be assigned an emergency station where you report for training and assessment. I wish I could tell you drills are a fascinating experience, but most of your time is spent standing around wishing you were still asleep in your cabin.

Guest Safety Briefing: after the Costa *Concordia* cruise ship sank, rules were put in place so that all guests must report to muster stations to review safety information before the ship leaves port. Crew with emergency duties report to their station to assist in the safety briefing. It's mostly a lot of standing around telling guests where to go but would be critically important in a real emergency.

Port Manning: this varies depending on the cruise line, but if you have to serve on "port manning" you don't have to do anything extra, you just can't leave the ship at a particular port or perhaps all ports for one cruise. It relates to the ship being required to have a minimum number of crew members on board at any given time for safety reasons. I have been on contracts where I served on port manning as often as every third cruise, as rarely as every sixth cruise, and sometimes not at all.

Embarkation Assistance: sometimes musicians are poached by the Guest Services department to assist guests during embarkation (when they first arrive on the ship). If your name comes up in the rotation, you will be stationed in a high-traffic area for 2-4 hours. In order to protect their voices for singing, it's not unusual for vocalists (including PBEs) to pay another crew member to take their place.

Other Dumb Stuff You Might Have to Do: the better PBE jobs are the ones where you are left alone to do what you do best—sell alcohol in the piano bar. But sometimes one of your supervisors comes up with a "brilliant" idea to involve the PBE in other scheduled events like:
1. **Shows:** on some ships you might be asked/required to be a part of a main-stage production show, jam session, or guest Q and A. Think of these events as promotion for your piano bar shows. The more guests that see you on the ship, the more possible traffic you'll attract to the piano bar.
2. **Musical games:** I've been on a couple of ships where I was required to host a "Name that Tune" contest and award prizes. Normally, such events are hosted by entertainment staff (not musicians), but EDs are always looking for ways to

add more events to the daily schedule without actually adding extra staff.
3. **Cocktail piano:** I have been scheduled to play background music for private parties outside of normal piano bar hours for things like guest-VIP acknowledgement parties, military appreciation gatherings, wedding receptions, and crew awards ceremonies. Playing "cocktail" music is not something all PBEs know how to do, so let your supervisor know what your comfort level is. In exchange for this performance, I didn't have to work as long that night in the piano bar, but that also meant less time to earn tips, so I try to get out of these extra sets whenever possible.

What Your Cabin Will Be Like: it is an industry wide standard that the PBE gets a private cabin. This is a perk most crew members, including the other musicians, don't have because cabin space is a valuable commodity. Additionally, you will have a cabin steward to make your bed each day, supply clean towels, and keep things clean. These people work very hard so tip them generously. Be prepared to be assigned a very small inner cabin (no windows) in a crew area, as opposed to a guest cabin. Cabins usually include a desk, shelf, chair, closet, hangers, phone, TV, and the smallest bathroom/shower you will ever see. Soap may or may not be available so bring your own to start. On my various contracts I have seen beds that were twins, fulls, and twin bunk beds. Sometimes a small refrigerator is provided, but you are not allowed to store any food or beverage in your cabin that could spoil. Older cruise ships don't have enough electrical outlets for modern needs so bring your own adapters and extension cords.

Cabin Inspections: once a month your cabin will be inspected for cleanliness and safety. Your immediate supervisor is usually with the inspectors and has already tipped you off about their arrival. This allows you time to hide your electrical adapters, cup warmers, wet food, and any other contraband. Toss everything in a drawer or closet during the inspection and put it back after they leave. It's silly, but that's how the game is played.

Practicing Your Music: this is always a challenge on a cruise ship. Port days while guests go ashore are the best time to practice in the piano bar. That means giving up your own time off the ship, but there may be no other choice. I have worked on ships where other pianos were sometimes available or small keyboards could be kept in your cabin, but you won't know for sure until you arrive. On my most recent contract, I was surprised to find a full-sized, 88-key, digital piano under the bed in my cabin.

Making Extra Money: if you want to pick up some extra cash while on a contract, there are several possibilities. The Art Department holds multiple auctions every cruise and usually hire musicians to help set up and tear down. The Photo Department often hires crew to act as costumed characters (pirates, waiters, etc.) for staged photos both on and off the ship. And if you are willing to give up time in ports, there are always crew members willing to pay for substitutes to cover their port manning or embarkation duties. I knew a highly driven guitarist who made at least $1,000 extra every month doing a smattering of all these jobs. I have personally found that I'd rather reserve my non-piano bar hours to write books, work on new songs, and allow my voice to recover, but additional money is available if you want it.

Crew Food: quality of crew food can vary widely between the cruise lines and even between ships of the same line. But overall, I have found the food to be consistently good with a variety of choices available. Most of the food in the crew area is served buffet style. Cruise ships often have 2-3 dining areas for crew. PBEs are allowed to eat in the Staff Mess or perhaps even the Officers Mess where there are usually table settings, items that can be ordered from a menu, and better décor. The Crew Mess (which is different from the Staff Mess) lacks niceties, but is open around the clock if you want a snack or hot beverage between standard meal times. Breakfast is served too early for most musicians to bother with, but the usual American breakfast items are available. At lunch and dinner there are several main and side dishes to choose from as well as salad bar, soup, and desserts. An effort is made to offer theme meals or special teas every couple of weeks. I have known many vegetarians on crew and they have less variety and sometimes supplement meals with outside food stored in their cabins. Protein powder is a popular commodity in crew areas.

Eating in Guest Areas: an important perk of being a PBE is access to guest areas which means you can eat outside of the crew dining rooms. Certain days or times are blacked out due to high guest-use, but being able to eat occasionally at the lido-deck buffet or café locations makes life much nicer. The drawback is that you are accessible to guests and in essence "on the clock," so be prepared to chat with people curious to have a moment with you outside the piano bar. A PBE gets used to hearing "Hey, Piano Man!" anytime he is walking around the guest areas of the ship.

The Truth About Ship Internet: the good news is that all cruise ships have internet. The bad news is that it is nothing like the speed you are used to having on land. Streaming video is choppy if not unwatchable. Messaging usually works better and is the primary way crew keep in touch. I have spent 10 minutes or more waiting for a couple of emails or web pages to open and sometimes just give up. Adding insult to injury, you will pay a per-minute charge while using the ship's internet. I have been told that some cruise lines have "pretty good" connection speeds, but I haven't personally witnessed such a thing.

Getting Laundry Done: stage clothes can be given to your cabin steward and they are returned from the laundry a day or two later washed and pressed. You'll wash personal clothes in a crew laundry for free (detergent is usually provided), but you may have to wait for machines to become available. I have yet to try this, but I have seen notices on several ships that the laundry department will also launder non-performance clothes for a nominal fee.

Religious Practice: it's not unusual to have 60 or more nationalities represented among crew and that also means a diversity in religions. There are no company-sponsored religious services for crew that I have ever seen, but I know crew take it upon themselves to create their own worship or prayer gatherings. One ship I was on had a small shrine used by crew.

The Five Offenses That Will Get You Fired: normally, if you do any of these things, you're going home at the next port, which may not be a convenient place to find your way home from:

1. **Fighting:** it doesn't matter who starts it, everyone involved goes home
2. **Stealing:** if you find something in a common area that isn't yours, do not take it to your cabin. Saying, "I was going to turn it in later," isn't an acceptable response. The items should be turned in to Security or the Crew Office.
3. **Drugs and Alcohol:** there is a zero tolerance for illegal drugs on cruise ships. On paper, no crew members are allowed to

drink while on duty, but PBEs are subject to a "look the other way" policy because making toasts and drinking are considered part of the job. However, be forewarned that if you have done something to turn your superiors against you, a breathalyzer test at the end of your show may be used to get you removed.
4. **Sexual Abuse:** committing any form of physical harm sends you home.
5. **Fraternizing with Guests:** PBEs get very familiar with guests, but be wary of crossing sexual lines. Without security clearance requested days or weeks in advance, you are never allowed in a guest cabin, nor are guests allowed in yours. I have heard of several examples of what is known as the "six o'clock knock" where security personnel are fully aware of a crew member spending the night in a cabin with a guest. During the night, security staff coordinate an action plan with the ED and MD. The guilty party gets an early knock on the cabin door and is told to pack their bags in front of a security officer before being escorted immediately to the gangway. You may seldom see them, but assume there are security cameras everywhere on a cruise ship tracking your movements.

Random Drug and Alcohol Testing: by working on a cruise ship you are agreeing to drug and alcohol testing. Supposedly, the crew are chosen at random, but I'm always suspicious that musicians seem to get targeted randomly more often than others. If you are selected, you will be notified to report immediately to the medical office where you will provide a urine sample. When I've been called for testing, the results were known before I walked away.

Visiting Ports and Taking Shore Excursions: entertainment booking agencies love to use exotic ports of call as an attractive tool to recruit new musicians. And while it's true you will travel to some beautiful places, you have to budget your shore time around ship-life realities. Guests are given first access to leave the ship and their "back on board" time might be 30 minutes longer than crew. So a five-hour port of call may only allow a four-hour window for you to get off and see the sights. Also, consider that port days are an excellent time to practice or eat in quiet guest areas. If I spend months doing the same route, I find that getting off the ship is fun for the first few weeks but less so after that. Shore excursions are occasionally offered just for crew at incredibly discounted prices, and I strongly encourage you to take part. If there is space remaining on a guest excursion you can likely get a discounted ticket for that as well. I've had amazing experiences river tubing in Jamaica, gasping at earth-divers in Vanuatu, being swarmed by parakeets in the Dominican Republic, and riding a train to the Alaskan frontier.

Getting Exercise: guests often complain that there is so much food available on their cruise that it is inevitable weight will be gained. The same problem faces the crew. With endless desserts, heavy sauces, and inexpensive alcohol available every day, it's easy to expand your waistline. Fortunately, forms of exercise are readily available to you. The crew usually have their own gym available 24 hours a day. In addition, PBEs should have access to the guest gym, although the hours may be limited. And most ships have an open-air jogging path on one of the open decks if you prefer being outside. As a backup plan, I travel with my own jump rope and workout resistance bands. Lastly, whenever you get off the ship I recommend you walk to your destination. You will benefit from the cardio and interact more closely with your surroundings.

Protip: I never use the elevators when I'm on a ship and burn a lot of calories without hardly trying.

Maintaining Vocal Health: here is a list of things I do to promote vocal health during my contracts. Pick and choose what works for you:

1. Vocal warm-up exercises: I do a series of scales and arpeggios using various vowel sounds every performance night for 30 minutes
2. No alcohol or soda during performances: I hydrate my voice with water or tea
3. Vocal rest during off hours: if my voice is strained, I avoid guest areas and seldom talk
4. Choose keys wisely: you don't get bonus points for performing in the original key of a song. If you are straining, lower the key. No one is keeping score.

Catching a Cold: sometimes I feel that a ship is a floating box of germs. Every handrail, door knob, kiosk, and handshake is a chance to get infected. I take daily doses of vitamin C and wash my hands often but still catch a cold at least once most every contract. As uncomfortable as it is, I tend to sing through a cold and just suffer for a few days so that I don't miss out on making tips. I go into damage-control singing mode that includes lowering the keys, clipping notes short that are usually sustained, playing longer instrumental sections, inviting guests to sing, and stretching breaks out as long as possible. But if I feel too sick to work, I can visit the medical center and get signed off for day or two. Guests might complain about no piano bar entertainment, but sometimes it can't be helped. If a PBE takes excessive time off due to medical reasons, the management may ask the home office to find a replacement.

Crew Bar and Your Social (Sex) Life: every ship I've been on had a bar just for crew. One ship even had two of them. This is the hub for social life among crew in their off hours. In the crew bar you will find comfortable furniture, a TV, a pool table, and the ever-popular inexpensive drinks (priced at about 25% of what you pay on land). There will likely be themed party nights and on special occasions one of the music acts might be scheduled to perform. As you can imagine, this is also where crew go if they are looking for physical relations. Cruise lines forbid crew-guest fraternization but fully support crew-crew relations. Condoms are usually provided free in the medical center and if you and a partner really hit it off, you can get your employer I.D. numbers "linked" so that you can be assigned a shared cabin. PBEs have less time for chilling in the crew bar because we usually work during the peak evening hours, but stopping by after the last show or on a night off is a common way to relax and maintain a social life.

All Bow Down to Guest Comments: the cruise lines are in serious competition with each other over market share and go to great lengths to gain a fraction of a percentage point in sales and customer satisfaction. As such, entertainment departments are often ranked within a fleet depending on the number of positive guest comments they receive. The entire industry is obsessed with getting guests to go on record about what they liked during a cruise and how likely they are to recommend the experience to others. More positive comments for the PBE can result in better treatment on the ship, first choice on future contracts, and pay raises. I suggest you take advantage of this by actively encouraging your guests to respond to their email surveys and say something about the good time they've had in the piano bar. I do it in a way that shifts the emphasis off of me by saying, "Hasn't the bartender been doing an excellent job this whole cruise?" While everyone applauds, I add, "When you get your email survey next week, you should take a little time to mention her name and how awesome she was in the piano bar. And if you want to add a little something about Piano Dude Gregg, that would be great." It never fails that while the other music acts on the ship receive two or three positive comments each cruise, I generate two or three pages. Granted, I'm putting on an excellent guest-oriented show, but the biggest reason I get so many more comments is simple: I ask for them. At the end of your contract, ask your MD if you can get a copy of all your guest comments. The best excerpts can be used when it's time to ask for a raise.

Protip: cruise lines seem to only email satisfaction surveys to the one person in a party who booked the cruise. In my observations, this person is usually a woman (the wife, mother, matriarch, etc.). So, do I place a slightly higher emphasis on keeping women in the piano bar entertained over men? Yes, I do. If cruise lines insist on making guest comments the coin of the realm, then I'm taking advantage of the system any way I can.

A Typical Schedule: when you work on a ship, one of the first things that happens is you no longer need to know what day of the week it is. Working towards the weekend or the concept of TGIF doesn't apply. The entire cruise is based on sea days and port days, not labels like Monday, Tuesday, or Wednesday. If you ask what day you can pick up your I.D. card the answer will something like, "Come by the crew office on Cozumel," (meaning the day the ship is in that port) or perhaps, "The second sea day." The MD will give you your schedule each cruise that breaks down your performance times for each day. The schedule might also include meetings or who has non-performance duties like port manning. You will be able to see the schedules for the other music acts and notice that they often have very scattered performances in different venues with large gaps between sets. Not so with the PBE because we perform solely in the piano bar and the starting time is nearly always the same. The other important item listed on your schedule is your night off. Typically, you are scheduled up to four hours of performance each night with one night off per week. One cruise line I worked for only required three sets per night but with zero nights off. In that case, I worked my entire five-month contract with only one night off granted me as a perk. Both systems have their advantages and after a few weeks you get used to whatever you have to do.

End-of-Contract Evaluations: one of the important tasks of the MD is to write end-of-contract evaluations for each of the musicians. If your contract is at least a few months long, you might also receive a mid-contract evaluation that allows you time to take action on managerial suggestions before you leave the ship. Depending on the cruise line, you will be assessed on categories including musicianship, showmanship, and off-stage qualities. As I emphasize throughout this book, musicianship is the least important category. Management is much more interested in the other two areas where guest interaction comes into place. You will never see a guest comment that says, "The PBEs use of the Lydian mode during his introduction to 'Friends in Low Places' was a fresh surprise that will result in my choosing this cruise line for all my future vacations." But comments like, "The PBE made us all feel like a family," or, "The piano bar offered the best entertainment on the ship," are entirely attainable and rated highly by your supervisor during evaluation time. Remember, the better you look, the better your boss looks. Take your evaluations seriously because they are often what leads to pay raises and getting first choice of future contracts.

Keeping Your Gig Is Easy

I'm going to be very honest with you: I've been made aware of some poor quality PBEs out there who keep finding work on cruise ships. That's not an excuse to accept mediocrity but an observation of what is happening in the real world. Like I explained in the Introduction, supply and demand favors the PBE at this point, so work is available if you want it. My strongest recommendation is to put on a show that is focused on positive guest interaction while spending your off-stage time accepting the realities of ship life and not being a jerk. Think you can handle that? If so, keeping your gig will be no problem.

CHAPTER 5: OVERVIEW OF THE CRUISE LINES

A fact many people find surprising is how few cruise line companies there are. Similar to the music industry where record companies merged and bought each other out over decades, there are a handful of major cruise line companies left standing. The largest is Carnival Corporation that owns about half of all the cruise ships in the world. The next largest, based on number of ships is Royal Caribbean, followed by Norwegian and MSC. Beyond that, there are a smattering of specialty cruise lines that focus on niche markets like sailing ships, river cruises, or high-end cruise experiences. The good news is that all the major cruise lines are expanding and constantly adding new ships. The largest growth is expected in China.

The cruise line industry is extremely fluid as far as entertainment goes, so whatever is programmed on a ship today may not be the case a year from now. Some of the piano bar-related changes include transitioning from acoustic pianos to digital, experimenting with the dueling piano bar format, and having the PBEs team up with other entertainers on the ship to present a more collaborative show. Fortunately, piano bars are still wildly popular and exist on most of the cruise ships in the world. The best I can do is to give you a current list of the various cruise lines with your understanding that the details could be different by the time you read this. You will need to do a little research on these companies to see who is hiring PBEs at any given moment (or ask a booking agent to find out for you). This list is current as of March 2022.

AIDA (owned by Carnival Corporation): 13 ships

Azamara (owned by Royal Caribbean Cruises Ltd): 4 ships

Carnival (owned by Carnival Corporation): 25 ships

Celebrity (owned by Royal Caribbean Cruise Ltd): 13 ships

Celestyal (owned by Louis group PLC): 2 ships

Costa (owned by Carnival Corporation): 10 ships

Cunard (owned by Carnival Corporation): 3 ships

Disney (owned by the Walt Disney Company): 5 ships

Fred Olsen (owned by Bonheur and Ganger Rolf): 4 ships

Hapag Lloyd (owned by TUI): 2 ships

Holland America (owned by Carnival Corporation): 11 ships

Marella (owned by TUI): 4 ships

MSC (owned by Mediterranean Shipping Company S.A.): 20 ships

Norwegian (owned by Norwegian Cruise Line Holdings Ltd): 19 ships

HOW TO BE AN AWESOME PIANO BAR ENTERTAINER ON CRUISE SHIPS

Oceana (owned by Norwegian Cruise Line Holdings Ltd): 7 ships

P & O (owned by Carnival Corporation): 7 ships

P & O Australia (owned by Carnival Corporation): 3 ships

Pheonix Reisen (owned by Pheonix Reisen): 4 ships

Princess (owned by Carnival Corporation): 15 ships

RSSC (owned by Norwegian Cruise Line Holdings Ltd): 6 ships

Royal Caribbean (owned by Royal Caribbean Cruise Ltd): 26 ships

Saga (owned by Saga Enterprises): 2 ships

Seabourn (owned by Carnival Corporation): 5 ships

SeaDream (owned by Atle Brynestad): 2 ships

Silversea (owned by the Lefebvres of Rome): 6 ships

Star Clippers (owned by Star Clippers Ltd.): 3 ships

TUI (owned by Royal Caribbean Cruise Ltd.): 7 ships

Viking (owned by Viking Cruise Ltd.): 9 ships

Virgin Voyages (owned by Virgin Group): 3 ships

Windstar (owned by the Anschutz Corporation): 6 ships

CHAPTER 6: AWESOME PROTIPS

I know you want to hear more about what it's really like performing as a PBE, so I'll share a bounty of my personal experiences with you that can be placed in one of two categories: performance or ship life. These are real-world topics that didn't necessarily fit into a previous chapter but are too important to leave out.

Protips for Being an Awesome Entertainer

Let the Guests Shine: after you've been a PBE for a while, you will start to see patterns in what guests say and do. The faces will be new, but it's all the same old bar-talk you've heard before. Even so, if a guest calls out to the room, "I bet nobody knows who wrote that song you just played," and you know darn well what the answer is, you're going to keep your mouth shut and let that guest have his moment. Or when a guest makes the same joke you've heard several times before, you're going to laugh louder than anyone in the room and declare your intentions to use that joke on all future cruises. And when guests yell, "bomp, bomp, bom" during the chorus of "Sweet Caroline" you're going to act like you've never been so delighted. The guests sitting in front of you may have been saving money a year or longer for their cruise and this is the one chance they get to live the life you experience months at a time. Don't do anything to diminish their moment to show off, be silly, or ask for the most cliché songs. When that loud-mouth guest comes through the piano bar door and shouts, "Sing us a song, you're the piano man," certain that he's the first one to ever be so clever, you will be thinking, "Here we go again," but what you'll do is smile and say, "Welcome friend; we've been waiting for you."

Timing Your Breaks: your exact start and end times may be decided for you with each set lasting 45-60 minutes. But often you are provided only a starting time and expected to keep a crowd entertained for up to four hours. In this situation, it is assumed that the PBE will adjust to the needs of the piano bar and take breaks only during lulls in the action. Sometimes I have played four hours straight with no break because the joint was jumping all night, and I didn't want to lose out on tips. Guests are typically very needy about being constantly entertained and the moment you take a break, they move on to the next lounge. However, if the crowd you have is proving tough to win over, taking a break and starting fresh with a new group of guests isn't a bad idea. Be wary that Entertainment Directors don't want you taking a break during peak transition times just after large events end elsewhere on the ship. Consult the daily schedule to avoid leaving the piano bar without entertainment at those moments.

Conversing with Guests: establishing personal connections with guests is easy by simply starting any conversation with "Where are you from?" or "Are you here celebrating a special occasion?" Then just listen and nod. Don't make it about you. An ice-breaking tactic I use on the first night of a cruise is to call out, "Who's here on vacation?" Naturally, everyone raises their hands, and I add, "Wow, we've already got a lot in common." Other topics you can ask about include that day's shore excursions, the weather back home, their favorite dessert in the dining room, or plans for the next port. Guests love thinking you are interested in their lives and by the end of the cruise it's typical for an awesome PBE to have created a family of regulars who spend most every evening in the piano bar getting to know each other. And truly, I have met people on ships with fascinating stories to tell.

Guests Asking Personal Questions: strangely, guests don't use the same social filters when talking with crew as they would with strangers back home. Being asked very personal questions about your life is a nightly occurrence. I find myself sometimes giving answers that are not exactly accurate because the specifics of my homelife are none of their business. You might even want to invent a "ship personality" to put some distance between overly inquisitive guests and your real life. Have a back-story all ready to go based on the personality you are willing to share with them.

Always Being "On" in Guest Areas: as a ship entertainer, you attract attention whenever you are in guest areas or even in port. This is part of the job so plan on always being polite and having a smile when approached. If you want to be left alone, you can always stay in the crew area of the ship.

The Best Answer for When You Don't Know a Request: never say "I don't know that song." Even though that's the simple truth, all it does is invite a questioning complaint from the guests like, "Why not?" or "Doesn't everyone knows that one?" Also, never suggest that you don't know a song because you think it's low quality. Even a song that seems moronic to you might have been the last song a guest's mother sang on her death bed. You never know.

The best answer when you don't know a request is to simply say, "I haven't learned that one yet." This suggests you *plan* to learn it at some point and their suggestion is somewhat affirmed as valid.

"Play Your Favorite Song:" I have received this request hundreds of times and sometimes it is presented strongly enough that it feels more like a demand. Guests feel like they are entitled to know this kind of personal information about you and expect an answer. Of course, any musician I know couldn't possibly have a single song that is their one and only favorite; it doesn't work that way. But if you try to explain that, guests think you're holding back. They are hoping you will reveal a secret to them you don't give out to others. Or perhaps they are trying to do you a favor by making a request where you get to fill in the song title of your own choosing. I have found the best response is to say, "Well, I don't have just one favorite, but I have a few songs that are always near the top of the list and here's one of them." Then I play a never-fail song like "Let It Be," "Imagine," or "Hallelujah." This type of response gives me wiggle room if another guest gives me $20 to play my "favorite song" 10 minutes later.

"Play My College Song:" I grew up in an area of California with no strong affiliation to a university sports program, so I was stunned when I moved elsewhere and learned what a huge part of daily life "game day" is. Guests bring their school spirit with them on a cruise and sometimes things get competitive around the bar as fans of opposing schools start jeering. Songs like "Sweet Home Alabama," and "Rocky Top" are not just innocent requests, they are statement-songs meant to rally allies and irritate the opposition. I usually find a way to exploit the situation for more tips, including being tipped to stop playing a song. I draw the line at playing actual school fight songs. For me, that's just too much trouble, and I'd rather focus on songs that everyone likes. I'm sure other PBEs have found a way to work fight songs into the act, but I'm not one of them. Whatever sells the alcohol.

Flipping the Gender in a Lyric: changing he to she or her to him in a song lyric is a long-accepted liberty taken by singers. It's entirely appropriate to make alterations like "I got a man, way over town; he's good to me," from "I Got a Woman" by Ray Charles or "I saw her standing there by the record machine" from "I Love Rock and Roll" by Joan Jett. I believe female PBEs are faced with singing most lyrics in their original form simply because the overwhelming majority of piano bar songs are from male artists. Flipping the genders in song after song may get tedious and sound confusing to the crowd. Each PBE, male or female, will have to decide what works best in their situation. As a male performer, I have decided to leave a few songs with strong female associations exactly as they were recorded so that the original viewpoint is left intact. This includes titles like "Jolene" from Dolly Parton, "Man, I Feel Like a Woman," from Shania Twain," and "Blank Space" from Taylor Swift.

Play Theme Sets: to create some buzz on the ship, ask the ED to include a themed set in the piano-bar schedule once or twice each cruise. This will also encourage the CD to mention you in daily announcements made around the ship. Themes you can try include: the music of a particular Broadway show or composer, Diva hits (this is particularly entertaining if you are a male PBE), or an all-request hour of one artist like the Beatles, Elton John, Billy Joel, Barbara Streisand, the Eagles, and the like (focusing on one artist for a full hour allows you the pleasure of playing material beyond the usual requested hits).

It's Okay to Shorten Songs: there is absolutely no law that says a PBE has to play complete versions of a song. Reasons to cut a song short include: it's not going over well with the crowd; you don't know the tune very well, but a request included a tip; you've already played the full song earlier; or a guest made the request without including a tip so they don't get all the verses.

Guests Asking to Perform with You: there are PBEs who go out of their way to invite guests to perform with them and make it a featured part of their act. This is an excellent way to preserve your own voice from overuse. But the downside is that the piano bar becomes just another venue for karaoke with a parade of amateur singers. This also excludes sing-alongs because the expectation with guest singers is that everyone else is supposed to listen politely and applaud rather than join in for a boisterous chorus. My solution when approached is to say that guests are welcome to sing a featured song the final night of the cruise. By then most of them have forgotten or they aren't real piano bar patrons so they don't come back.

Guests Asking If You Know Their Favorite PBE: a common occurrence is that guests come into the piano bar on the first night of a cruise and promptly announce they are "serious" piano bar fans, proclaim who their favorite PBE is, and expect you to know who they are talking about. This is one of the moments you have to be very comfortable with who you are as a PBE. Don't get caught up trying to compete with a PBE who's not in the room and you will likely never meet. When guests say to me, "My favorite PBE does lots of silly songs about farm animals; you should do those too," I have to calmly remind myself to just do what I do. I also take comfort in thinking that the farm animal PBE is on another ship at that very moment where a guest is saying, "You should be more like that Piano Dude Gregg; he's awesome."

Drunk and Unruly Guests: I'm fortunate to have only called on security one time to remove an inebriated guest from the piano bar. A very drunk man brought his own full-sized tambourine with him and started throwing it across the piano at other guests without warning. People were going to be hurt, so I stopped playing and made the call. For the regular variety of drunk, loud guests, I usually start by trying to engage them in conversation over the mic and hope that the attention calms them down. If they get to the point where other guests are starting to leave, I take a break and step out of the room. Drunk people like being where they think the action is and will move on. The other guests pick up on what I'm doing and appreciate it. Half the time the offending guest comes back another night, apologizes for their behavior, and we have a laugh about it.

Guests Who Invade Your Personal Space: unfortunately, some piano bars are designed in a way that leaves you vulnerable to guests getting right next to you while you play. I have had to keep my cool while guests do various combinations of the following: forcibly sit next to me on the piano bench, unbutton my shirt, place their hands under my shirt, give me uninvited kisses on my cheeks and neck, rub my head, and move my hat from my head to theirs. This kind of intrusion is very unsettling and has creeped me out to the point of hardly being able to continue performing. If I ever did any of those things to a guest, I'd be fired, period. But guests do it to the PBE and it is considered "just having fun." It's not fair, but it's the reality you might face. Protect yourself as much as possible and stay aware of your surroundings. Try to set up other equipment or furnishings to block easy access to where you sit. Ask the bar staff to help fend off invasive guests. You'll probably even find that other guests are on your side and offer to help. If a problem occurs, it's always your right to announce, "I need to take a break and will be back soon." Confronting the offending guest may be unavoidable (I have threatened to call security several times), but try to walk out with no further interaction. Let your supervisor know what happened and emphatically state that you expect something to be done to stop it in the future.

Double-Dipping Requests for the Same Song: if several request slips pile up on your piano, it's not unusual that some of them will list the same song. When you play that song, don't acknowledge any guest by name. Simply say, "The next song is an extra special request, and I'm glad to play it for you." This way all the guests who made the request believe you are playing it for them. You are essentially double-dipping the same song to garner appreciation (and hopefully tips) from multiple parties.

Broken Piano Strings: if your ship has an acoustic piano, plan on breaking strings. I had never broken a piano string in my life until I became a PBE. Now, one or two broken strings per contract is the norm. The pianos are played hard nightly for years and even if you have a light touch, you can break a string the previous PBE took to the brink. Let your Music Director know immediately which string is broken so they can email the piano technician before their next scheduled visit. This allows the tech to bring exactly the right strings rather than having to wait another 2-4 weeks until they return.

Dealing with Slow Nights: through no fault of your own you might have nights in the piano bar with few guests. I have been on cruises with popular early morning shore excursions that keep guests from staying out late the night before which means the piano bar is lightly attended. Other nights there are so many entertainment options for guests like main shows, comedians, the night club, and deck parties that it's hard to gather much of a crowd in the piano bar. When that happens, and it will, don't take it personally. Just say to the crowd you have, "Well, it looks like we're down to only the cool kids" and play some tunes you don't get around to very often. Consider setting the microphone aside and striking up conversation with the guests sitting nearby. Turn a slow night into an intimate conversation among new friends. Take advantage of the fact that you can play unusual songs or try new ones, and get to know some interesting people.

Plan for Holidays and Special Occasions: when you get a contract, be sure to look ahead on the calendar to see what holidays occur while you are on the ship. Gather related songs, clothes, costume items, or decorations ahead of time and bring them with you. Just as importantly, check the calendar for important dates in your private life like family birthdays and anniversaries and plan ahead for how you will acknowledge them.

An Electric Fan: some PBEs get extremely hot while performing; if that is your tendency, purchase a small electric fan at a port and keep it under the piano. Unless you have extra space in your baggage, plan on leaving the fan for the next PBE at the end of your contract. You might also try asking House Keeping if they have a fan to loan you.

Getting Along with Bar Staff: the first night of your contract be sure to introduce yourself to the staff in the piano bar and learn their names. These people will have your back if you treat them right. Mention them over the microphone when you see them working hard. Get the crowd to give them a round of applause now and then. If you hear one of them singing, ask if they want to perform a song sometime. Guests love to see "spontaneous" collaboration they feel is unique to their cruise. You and the bar staff have a symbiotic relationship. If you keep the room full of guests, they make tips; and if the bar staff is doing a great job serving drinks, the guests are easier to entertain and you make tips. You all have the same goal to sell alcohol and earn some money so make friends and team up.

Protips for Mastering Ship Life

Packing Hacks: some things I've found handy for living on a ship include: zip lock bags, a multi-tool, rubber bands, a hot-beverage cup with lid, postage stamps and envelopes, back-up chargers for devices, a laundry bag, soft tissues (the kind on the ship feel like sandpaper on the nose when you have a cold), an external speaker for your laptop, and two pair of ear buds because you're sure to lose or break one of them.

Maintaining Relationships on Land: this single issue is the downfall of many crew members and leads to them not pursuing future contracts. Romantic relationships become strained, children in your life grow up without you, and your dog growls at you like a stranger when you come home. Plan on spending considerable amounts of money staying in touch. Ask other crew if there are ports with free internet. You might also get an international plan so your phone will work in various ports. And phone cards are available on the ship that allow you to make calls from your cabin phone. Use some or all of these methods to reach out to loved ones back home as much as possible. It will still be hard being so far away, but you'll miss family a little less.

Dating Crew Members: during a question and answer panel with ship guests, I heard a cruise director humorously describe dating between crew members as a first date that never ends because you'll see each other at breakfast, lunch, and dinner until the end of a contract whether you want to or not. Such close proximity is not a normal feature of dating on land where you have the opportunity for "alone time." If the relationship is strong, the closeness is a bonus, but if things don't work out, you'll still be seeing each other constantly. This is a recipe for drama and tense emotions so try to enter into dating relationships only when both parties seem mature enough to handle the possible outcomes. PBEs have shorter contracts than most other crew members so be prepared to leave others behind and consider how this will affect all those concerned.

Getting Paid and Paying Taxes: there will be variety among the cruise lines as to how and when you will receive your salary. I have been paid via auto-deposit every two weeks by one company while another paid in cash only once a month. Either way, there will be a delay of at least a few weeks before you receive your first salary, so plan on bringing a little spending cash to tide you over until you make some tips. If you are an American, be prepared for Federal taxes to be withheld from your salary (for me, the deduction has usually been 12-15%). State taxes will be paid by you at tax time and there isn't any getting out of it because you will most likely receive a W-2 as an employee.

Extension Cords and AC Adapters: these items are not allowed in your cabin, but everyone has them. You'll want them too.

Gaming Systems and Video: many of the veteran ship musicians I know bring their own game systems and hard drives full of video with them on contracts. These items help fill the hours on long sea days.

Crew Excursions and Discounts: the Crew Office and HR department will keep you informed of special events for crew and you should partake whenever possible. You can save big money over standard prices and have some fun off the ship. I once paid $10 for an excellent Alaskan excursion that cost guests $150. It's also good policy to ask any business you visit in port if they offer crew discounts. Even if they don't have an official discount, taking 10% off your bill is common. You won't know if you don't ask.

Laundry Hacks: if you aren't present when your washing or drying cycle ends, be prepared to find that someone else has moved your clothes out of the way because machines are in high demand. Detergent and softener should be available for free, so I usually grab a handful of the little boxes at the beginning of my contract and keep them in my cabin. On my contracts, I try to bring as many clothing items as possible that are wrinkle resistant and dry quickly. It will save you dryer and ironing time.

Video of Problems in Your Cabin: one time I had a cabin with a flooding problem and I let the Crew Office know within the first few days of my arrival. A series of technicians all came, shrugged their shoulders, and said, "Not my department." Weeks went by and the problem got worse. One morning, I awoke to a bathroom full of black water overflowing into the cabin area. I whipped out my phone to video the event as it happened. Showing this video proof to the Crew Office staff minutes later got them jumping. I was given a temporary cabin while the drains were snaked, new concrete was poured, and tile were replaced. This all happened because they didn't dare want to see that video I had get posted online. If you have problems in your cabin you don't like, a verbal complaint backed up with video proof carries serious weight.

Name Tags: most the cruise lines require the PBE to wear a name tag whenever you are in a guest area. You will be provided one or two when you arrive for your first contract. I buy a couple extra because it's nice to leave them attached to various garments you often wear. I designate one for formal clothes, one for standard performance clothes, one for daytime clothes, and one for workout shirts.

Making Friends and Allies Among Crew: you will find that crew tend to self-affiliate within their own tribe. At the dining rooms and crew bar you will see dancers, musicians, audio techs, etc. all sitting in their own groups. It makes sense because these are the people with shared interests. But be sure to mix it up and meet crew from other departments. Some of the most interesting conversations will happen sitting with a stranger from India, Serbia, the Philippines, Brazil, St. Lucia, Vanuatu, and all points in between. Always offering a pleasant "hello" to management is an easy way to keep them on your side down the road. Furthermore, being friendly with the staff outside the entertainment department can save you countless headaches when problems arise. Several of my non-musician crew mates wonderfully stepped up for me once when my wife's flight was delayed by three hours on the day she was scheduled to join me for a cruise. I had people from Guest Services all the way up to the Captain offering assistance to get her on the ship before we sailed. They really came through for us and might not have done so had they found me an unpleasant person to work with. To sum up, smile and don't be a jerk.

Family Sailing with You: this is one of the best perks available while working on a ship. Family and friends can sail with you at a substantial discount. If your cabin has sleeping space for two, you can have a guest stay with you for nearly free (I have paid as little as $7 per day). Otherwise, if a guest cabin is available, your family can sail for as little as $30 a day (per person). While your family is sailing, you can request privileges to eat with them in the guest-only dining rooms for little or no charge. And when you want to take your own cruise between contracts, 30% discounts are not unusual for crew members. Then you will have the opportunity to head straight for the piano bar and watch one of your peers in action.

Staying Healthy: I go for the holistic approach and try a little of everything to not get sick. I use the gym 5-6 times a week, eat simple meals without sauces and added sugar, avoid alcohol, wash my hands frequently, take vitamin C supplements, and try to get enough sleep by avoiding the crew bar. Even with all that, I usually catch a cold at least once on every contract. There are just too many people with too many germs in the same confined space when working on a ship. Do what you can to live a healthy life, but bring some cold medicine with you all the same.

Getting Sea Sick: my first PBE contract was also the first time I had ever been on a cruise ship. We sailed some very rough waters in the Coral Sea, and I spent much of the first month horribly sea sick. There were performances where I would take a break, go to my cabin and throw up, then return to the piano bar minutes later for another set. It was rough going, to say the least. But one day I woke up feeling better and that was the end of it; no more motion sickness. If you're not sure how your body will react to being at sea for days at a time, bring whatever remedy you think will be helpful.

I see many guests using the patch behind the ear and swear by it. Others use the wrist band. I've spoken to crew members with over 10 years' experience who still take sea sickness pills once in a while.

If Money is Your Priority, Avoid Drydocks and This Type of Cruise: Cruises longer than 10 days attract older crowds who don't typically tip as much. You might enjoy the interesting itinerary and having more time to know guests, but the money will be lower than a short cruise. Make sure you are comfortable with that knowledge on the front end. Also, if a ship is being renovated in drydock, you don't make tips at all for those days, the food is limited, ventilation to cabins and water service is intermittent, and you're probably in a port with few amenities. I avoid any contract that involves a drydock.

Fraternizing with Guests: part of your job is to engage the guests through song, banter, comedy, and conversation. If you do your job well, the lines may get blurry for your piano bar fans. There are guests who spend every night of the cruise sitting right next to you and by the end of the week consider themselves your intimate acquaintances. On the last night, they will ask for photos with you and want hugs goodbye. That's as far as you ever want it to go. Do not exchange phone numbers or home addresses. Do not tell them the names of your spouse and children. Do not call a cabin number if a guest includes it on a request slip. Do not agree if they want a picture of them kissing you or any other overly familiar form of contact. Just say, "Crew members aren't allowed to do that," and take a step back. This chips away at their perception of the relationship they think they have with you, but it can't be helped. You do your job, and at the end of the week the guests have to do their job, which includes letting go of any escape fantasies they've created. Early on, I made a few exceptions to my own suggestions and got away with it, but I've heard from other PBEs who made the exact same exceptions with horrible results. I'm much more careful now and feel fortunate that I didn't have to learn a lesson the hard way.

CHAPTER 7: YOUR LONG-TERM CAREER PLAN

Working on a cruise ship is not a good fit for many musicians; the challenges of ship life are plentiful, and many talented musicians either get fired, are not asked back, or choose not to pursue future contracts. But remember, the difficulty of the job is a good thing because the high turn-over rate is what contributes to PBE supply verses demand coming out in your favor. If the job was too easy, there would be an abundance of workers for the cruise lines to select from and the pay would go down. The work is just hard enough to cull the recruitment pool and leave room for motivated individuals like you.

I can often be heard saying to guests in the piano bar that I have the best job on the ship and it's no joke. The number of hours I actually spend "on the clock" in relation to salary makes the job of cruise ship PBE a fabulous way to make a living. Throw in the other perks like travel, discounts, food, and lodging, and it only gets better. But one of the greatest advantages of working as a PBE I haven't said much about yet is the potential for wealth-building. A successful PBE should take advantage of the financial gains available and fold them into a long-term career plan. Here are some considerations.

Financial Goals

You may not be the type to have your entire financial life laid out, but at least plan for what you will do with the income earned during your first contract. Two common financial mistakes I often see from crew members on first contracts is to overspend and not have any work on the books for when they go home. This leads to not having as much money as they hoped for at the contract's end and quickly burning through their reserves because of not having any gigs waiting on land. Consider setting a savings goal and put aside money from each paycheck. Give yourself a limited budget for ship-life items like internet and drinks in the crew bar. Avoid eating off the ship when meals in the crew area are free. In the meantime, keep up relationships with business contacts back home so that you have some work between ship contracts.

Years at Sea

After you work a few contracts, start pondering how many years you are comfortable working at sea. I've seen many crew members with 5-10 years of ship work tell me, "I took this job for one summer after college, and I'm still here." Some of them love the work. Unfortunately, there are others who really don't want to still be living the crew life but can't come up with a better plan. They just assumed early on that a better opportunity would present itself, and until it does they will "just work one more contract." In order to stay more content with your life, I suggest setting a limit for the number of years you will work on cruise ships before you have met your goals and can move on. You can always extend your personal contract, but it's good to have an end-date in mind. Saying, "I'm doing this gig until I can pay cash for a car" is much better for your state of mind than working with no end-game.

Goals for Marriage and Family

Obviously, wanting to be married and raise children is a substantial factor when considering your long-term career as a PBE. Having family and being a PBE are not exclusive, but they do present challenges. I see non-PBE crew members work 7-9 month contracts and watch their kids grow up via Skype, and I don't know how they can stand being away. Many cruise lines push for PBE contracts of at least four months, but for me personally, I have decided to only work for about two months at a time and then I spend another two months at home with my family. My wife cruises with me when her schedule allows, and this is an arrangement we have been able to manage. But it means there are potential longer contracts I cannot work. That's a tradeoff for wanting to maintain my relationships with family at home, and as a PBE you will have to find a balance that works for you.

Working for Cruise Lines on Land

Those of you with management skills might be interested in following the path I've seen many ship musicians take towards working at the "home office" after several years at sea. This usually involves moving to Miami where many cruise lines have corporate facilities. Jobs such as Music Supervisor, Casting Director, or Special Projects Manager allow you to stay connected with the cruise line industry and friends you've made, but you can live at home with a family while you do it.

Retirement Plans and Bonus Payments

When you first get hired by a cruise line you will be informed of their job benefits for crew members who stay with the company for many years. If you're young-ish, you may not bother listening because talk of retirement seems so irrelevant, but I can't tell you how many times I've heard a crew member with several years of experience say, "I wish I had paid attention and asked more questions." Because cruise lines are not strictly American businesses (even though they have American offices), they don't offer what Americans think of as conventional retirement plans. There are likely no pensions or 401K accounts. But your company may offer access to stock purchase programs, Individual Retirement Accounts, and payroll deductions to help you meet savings goals. Other cruise lines might offer a bonus payment based on a percentage of salary for crew members who work 10 years or more. Bonus payments may require a minimum number of days worked each year so be sure to ask questions until you understand exactly how the program works.

Have a Plan for "After"

I recently had a conversation with another ship musician who had just passed his tenth year with one cruise line and received a substantial bonus payment. This is the point in life when most crew members step away from the job, so I asked him what his plans were for the future. He's in his late 30s, and I was surprised to hear his answer: "I don't really have anything going on, so I guess I'll just do another contract." He wasn't going to take another contract because he *wanted* to but because he *had* to. Even after 10 years to come up with a plan, he hadn't saved much money or thought about what would come next. Working over a decade at sea is great if that's what you want to do, but if not, come up with an exit strategy. Take classes online along the way, read lots of books on early retirement, learn the basics of making financial investments, investigate small business opportunities, come up with a timeline to pay off a house, or make connections so you can move into management. Whatever you do, *don't do nothing* and just let the years tick by. In the blink of an eye you'll be 10 years older, no richer, and possibly no wiser. Make the most of the amazing personal and financial opportunities being a PBE offers you.

CHAPTER 8: AN EVENING IN THE LIFE OF PIANO DUDE GREGG

I survey the room while tinkling on the piano keys. Chat up the retired college educators from Pennsylvania and share I used to be a professor. Offer a friendly nod to the pleasant Corvette-owning couple that has come in every night and knows I have a Zo6. Give a wink to the Captain's teenage daughter sailing with us this week who quickly flashes her brace-filled smile at me: she'll be a knock out in years to come. Welcome by name the husband-wife from South Carolina who I stopped near the pool earlier to reveal I had learned a song request just for them. Take a moment to connect with the two 40-something wives whose husbands have moved on to the casino. Observe the young-ish couple sitting in the dark corner sweetly holding hands. Take note that the big spender from Kansas isn't in yet, but he likes to make an entrance later in the night. Oh yeah, these and the other dozen people around the room make up a crowd I can work with. Check the lights, adjust my hat, tip the microphone, and it's business time.

"Ain't No Mountain High Enough" to start: a do-no-harm song that everybody likes but wouldn't likely request on their own. A piano bar entertainer never plays an A-list song without a request: don't waste the money makers.

While playing, I begin my routine of scan and smile. Start to my far left. If it's a couple, always look at the lady first. Catch her eyes until she smiles, return the gesture and hold that moment just a second longer so she knows I really am looking at her, then move to her partner and give him a respectful "You're a lucky man" look. Scan to the next group and start over. Older couple? Make sure I play some Elvis soon. College girls on spring break? Some Taylor Swift will have them gleefully singing along. The working man in a t-shirt and ball cap sitting with his 50-something wife who looks 65 from her years of hard decisions and cigarettes? Bob Seger and Tom Petty on the way. Smile and scan. A family reunion from Utah? I'll learn the name of the loudest and say, "Here comes trouble" when they bring up a request, making them all laugh with delight to think of themselves as rowdy. Smile and scan. The couple who dress exceptionally nice for their evening out? Clapton's "Wonderful Tonight" will do just fine as I say, "This one is for the ladies who put a little extra time into getting ready tonight." If the guy is smart, he'll ask her to slow dance and tip me for knowing I just got him some action later that night. A 20th wedding anniversary shared with friends? A 30th birthday for a young mother free of the kids for a night? The solo hipster-guy who thinks I should play more obscure music he likes instead of popular music everyone else likes? Excellent. Smile and scan.

I see you all. I acknowledge you all. While you sit here in front of me you have worth, you matter, you belong, and in another life we would have been the closest of friends, lovers, siblings, soul mates and confidants. Smile and scan. A request for "Sweet Caroline" in the first five minutes? What a bold party animal you are. "Don't Stop Believing" is your favorite song? Of course it is, and no one has ever sung along about that small-town girl with as much conviction. "Piano Man," you say? Well, I usually save that song for later, but you're such an awesome crowd that I'm going to break my rule and play it for you right now. A $20 bill for playing the song I said I learned for you even though I already knew it? A $10 tip for keeping your wife occupied while you finished watching the game in your cabin? A $5 casino chip for playing "Joy to the World" a second time in 15 minutes? A $1 tip for a request slip with 10 songs on it? Requests for "anything Elton," "anything Adele," or "anything Billy Joel?" Bring it on. I've got you covered good people. "Please play YOUR favorite song?" Well, now we have a problem because I don't perform my favorite songs in public, but such details are inconvenient, so I'll break out "Let It Be" and we're good to go.

Then the questions come, as they always do. "Where are you from?" "How long are you here?" "And you live on the ship the whole time?" "You don't have a real job back home?" "Family?" "How does your wife feel about this?" I jubilantly provide answers because surely normal social boundaries don't apply to such intimate acquaintances as us.

When the evening concludes, I graciously accept platitudes as I gather my disco-ball sunglasses, feather boas, drink-splattered song lists, and crumpled dollar bills scattered across the piano lid. "You are the best entertainer on the ship." "We've been on 7 cruises and you're our favorite piano man." "If only we'd found you sooner, we would have come every night." "Do you ever perform near Dayton?" Always with sincerity I respond: Thank you; You're very kind; I really appreciate it; I'm sure it's very nice there.

And then there's the one who lingers because she's sure we've developed a bond over our several nights together. It's been years since anyone has paid her as much attention, called her by name, told her she looks nice, and simply looked her in the eyes and smiled.... And my dear, you are right to want that, crave that, and finally receive that. If it feels special, then it is, and you can have that feeling forever if you choose. But it's late, the lights have dimmed, and it's time for me to leave.

Tonight was beautiful, joy-filled, and a rarity that may never be matched, but it was also just like any other night, and tomorrow it all *starts over. Check the lights, adjust my hat, tip the microphone...business time.*

--"Piano Dude" Gregg Akkerman
May 2018

APPENDIX 1: BOOKING CONTACTS

Booking agencies come and go often enough that any list I provide here will certainly become dated and less useful over time. When in doubt, always consult with other cruise ship musicians you know and ask for referrals. Also, search online and do what you can to find out the background of the booking agencies you find. Many are excellent, some less so. But remember, any agency that requests an upfront fee is to be avoided. That's simply not how reputable booking agencies run a business. They get paid when you get paid.

As of 2018, here are some agencies (listed alphabetically) that either I have used, acquaintances have used, or appear to be reputable because of my awareness of them over a span of time. I'm sure there are other agencies out there that are wonderful, but these are the ones I feel comfortable listing at the moment. Always do your own research and ask lots of questions.

The Entertainment Agency
172 Main Street, Spencer, MA 01562-2117, USA
Phone: 508-885-6911
Email: enquiries@entagency.com
Website: http://www.entagency.com/pianogigs

Landau Music
924 Valley Avenue
Solana Beach, CA 92075
Email: info@landaumusic.com
Website: https://www.landaumusic.com/

Lime Entertainment
15 Wood Avenue, Ardsley, NY, USA
Phone: 914-393-8094
Email: auditions@limemusicentertainment.com
Website: http://www.limemusicentertainment.com

Suman Entertainment Group
12426 West Dixie Highway, Unit A
North Miami, FL 33161
Phone: 305-981-3135
Email: ewormsbaker@sumanent.com
Website: http://sumanent.com/

ProShip Entertainment
42 Reads Way, New Castle, DE 19720-1649, USA
Phone: 888-882-0996
Email: info@proship.com
Website: http://www.proship.com

APPENDIX 2: PACKING LIST

What's listed below is the actual list I print out before every 8-week contract and then check off as I pack and prepare to leave. Obviously, a woman will want to include items that don't apply to me, and I'm also bald so you'll notice I don't include hair products. I'm able to fit all these items in a large suitcase that is checked as luggage at the airport, and a backpack and shoulder bag that I carry on the plane. The suitcase usually contains all my clothes, health, and personal items, and weighs about 48-50 pounds which is right at the limit to avoid being charged an extra fee by the airlines. Everything else goes in my carry-on bags. This list works for me and will give you a starting point as you customize it to your needs.

Performance Clothes
   Black shoes
   Porkpie Hat
   Black shirts (4)
   White shirt (1)
   Vests (1-2)
   Black slacks (1-2)
   Black jeans (2)
   Dress belt
   Ties (2)
   Tie Chain

Dress socks (10 pr.)
Holiday items?
Name tags (4)
Lanyards (2)

Off-Duty Clothes
Day shoes
Flip flops
Sunglasses
Eye glasses
Ball cap
Casual belt
T-shirts (3)
Underwear
Hoodie
Light jacket
Heavy coat (depending on itinerary)
Collared shirts (3)
Shorts (2)
Swim suit
Beach towel
Ankle socks (6 pr.)
Workout clothes
Sleeping clothes
Blue jeans

Health/Hygiene
Tooth-paste
Breath mints
Tooth-brushes
Floss/pics
Lotion

Mouth-wash
Bar soap (2)
Razors
Manicuring scissors
First-aid kit
Pain reliever
Deodorant
Prescriptions
Supplements
Cold medicine

Personal Items
Money clip with traveling cash, ID, and credit cards
Jump rope
Resistance bands
Workout gloves
Cup w/lid
Travel food
Writing surface
Travel office kit
Multi-tool
Cards/stamps
Laundry bag
Zip-lock bags
Framed picture of wife
Clock

Technology
iPad w/chargers
iPhone w/charger
Laptop w/charger, mouse, speaker
Jump drive

Flashlight
Microphone
1-to-3 AC adapter
Extension chord
Ear buds
Piano key
Tuning wrench
Harmonicas (2)

Stage Gear
Social media sign
Song lists
Kazoo
Elton glasses
CDs
Foot Tambourine
Tip-jar basketball hoop
$20 in small bills to seed the tip jar
Neil Diamond scarf

Important Documents
Medical docs
Passport
Letter of employment
Training proofs
CD sales approval
Plane ticket
Hotel info
Boarding info

Preparation Checklist
Cover the car

Leave keys on dashboard
Travel cash ($100)
Make sure financial accounts and bills are current
Backup/update all devices
Check-in/seat assignment
Verify hotel booking

APPENDIX 3: SONG LISTS

I could provide you lists of thousands of songs, but you'll be better served by quality over quantity. Therefore, I'll focus on several hundred tunes that have proven night after night to be crowd-pleasers and what I think of as "do no harm" songs. One of the major cruise lines provides guests of the piano bar with a printed list of 100 choice songs, so I will fold them into my list as well. The 50 "need to know" songs from Chapter 1 are also included. Collectively, these are titles that many people love, most people like, nearly everyone recognizes, and almost no one hates. A perfect example would be "My Girl." You really can't go wrong playing that song because no one can legitimately stomp out of the room frustrated by your crappy choice.

You'll notice I avoid slow, sad love songs. Tunes like "I Will Always Love" and "Tears in Heaven" are great songs, but that doesn't mean they're great piano bar songs where you are trying to keep the energy up and (never forget) SELL ALCOHOL in a fun and interactive environment. Even if I can play some of those downer songs, I never include them in a list given to guests because they (and let's be honest, when I say "they" I mean women) will immediately ask for the slowest, saddest song on the list even though the mood in the room is "let's party." Now you're stuck either playing a song you shouldn't or offending a guest by telling her she has made a choice that is tone deaf to the spirit of the moment. Remove the problem by not including such songs on your hand-out list. Sad songs can be played if it's a smaller, mellow crowd, but remember, it's okay to say "no" if you don't think a request serves the bigger picture.

There are also many songs and genres that appeal to regional areas and tastes (New Orleans for instance), but in this list I'm focusing on songs that work across larger demographics. Lastly, you may have an excellent voice for more stylized genres like contemporary R & B, heavy metal, hip-hop, Texas country, or your own originals, but those are songs that should fill out the edges of your PBE song list, not dominate it. I'll hand you the meat and potatoes, and you decide how much spice to add as your own master song list continues to grow.

You really can't go wrong learning all these songs, but prepare to learn hundreds more based on your own expertise, the expectations of your employer, and (most importantly) the requests you get from the crowd. They'll let you know in a hurry where the weaknesses are in your song list. Learning every song on this list might take you years, but think of it as a valuable task that never really ends. Suggestions on how to efficiently learn songs are in Appendix 5.

Songs Awesome Cruise Ship PBEs Should Know: The Expanded List

Songs Since 2010
    "All of Me" by John Legend
    "Blank Space" by Taylor Swift
    "Forget You" by Cee Lo Green
    "Havana" by Camila Cabello
    "I Will Wait" by Mumford and Sons

"Moves Like Jagger" by Maroon 5
"Perfect" by Ed Sheeran
"Queen of California" by John Mayer
"Rolling in the Deep" by Adele
"Shake It Off" by Taylor Swift
"Sign of the Times" by Harry Styles
"Stay with Me" by Sam Smith
"Telephone" by Lady Gaga
"Thinking Out Loud" by Ed Sheeran
"Uptown Funk" by Bruno Mars
"When I Was Your Man" by Bruno Mars

2000s
"All Summer Long" by Kid Rock
"Bartender Song" by Rehab
"Bright Lights" by Matchbox 20
"Californication" by Red Hot Chili Peppers
"Chariot: by Gavin DeGraw
"Clocks" by Coldplay
"Drops of Jupiter" by Train
"Haven't Met You Yet" by Michael Bublé
"I'm Outta Time" by Oasis
"If I Had $1,000,000" by Bare Naked Ladies
"Ignition (Remix)" by R Kelly
"It's My Life" by Bon Jovi
"Mr. Brightside" by the Killers
"Party in the USA" by Miley Cyrus
"Picture" by Kid Rock/Sheryl Crow
"Rehab" by Amy Winehouse
"Single Ladies" by Beyoncé
"Viva la Vida" by Coldplay

1990s
"1979" by Smashing Pumpkins
"3 a.m." by Matchbox 20
"Baby Got Back" by Sir Mix-A-Lot
"Candle in the Wind" by Elton John
"Closing Time" by Semisonic
"Creep" by Radiohead
"Enter the Sandman" by Metallica
"Everything I Do I Do It for You" by Bryan Adams
"Free Fallin'" by Tom Petty
"Friday I'm in Love" by the Cure
"Gin and Juice" by Snoop Dog
"Hallelujah" by Jeff Buckley
"Home Sweet Home" by Mötely Crüe
"I'd Do Anything for Love" by Meat Loaf
"Kiss from a Rose" by Seal
"No Diggity" by Blackstreet
"November Rain" by Guns 'n' Roses
"Santeria" by Sublime
"Smells Like Teen Spirit" by Nirvana
"That's Just the Way It Is" by Bruce Hornsby
"Time of Your Life" by Green Day
"Truly Madly Deeply" by Savage Garden
"Walking in Memphis" by Marc Cohn
"Wannabe" by the Spice Girls
"What's Up (I Said Hey)" by 4 Non Blonds
"Wonderwall" by Oasis

1980s
"Against the Wind" by Bob Seger
"Allentown" by Billy Joel
"America" by Neil Diamond

"Blister in the Sun" by Violent Femmes
"Careless Whisper" by George Michael
"Come on Eileen" by Dexy's Midnight Runners
"Don't Stop Believing" by Journey
"Easy Like Sunday Morning" by Lionel Ritchie
"End of the Innocence" by Don Henley
"Every Rose Has Its Thorn" by Poison
"Faithfully" by Journey
"Fight for Your Right to Party" by Beastie Boys
"Five Hundred Miles (I'm Gonna Be)" by the Proclaimers
"Footloose" by Kenny Loggins
"Glory Days" by Bruce Springsteen
"Have I Told You Lately" by Van Morrison/Rod Stewart
"Hello" by Lionel Ritchie
"Here I Go Again" by Whitesnake
"Hit Me with Your Best Shot" by Pat Benatar
"Hurt So Good" by John Mellencamp
"I Just Called to Say I Love You" by Stevie Wonder
"I Love Rock 'n' Roll" by Joan Jett
"I Still Haven't Found What I'm Looking For" by U2
"I'm Still Standing" by Elton John
"It's Still Rock and Roll to Me" by Billy Joel
"Jack and Diane" by John Mellencamp
"Jenny 867-5309" by Tommy Tutone
"Keep Your Hands to Yourself" by the Georgia Satellites
"Kiss" by Prince/Tom Jones
"Kokomo" by Beach Boys
"Little Red Corvette" by Prince
"Mainstreet" by Bob Seger
"Mony, Mony" by Billy Idol
"Never Gonna Give You Up" by Rick Astley
"New York State of Mind" by Billy Joel

"Only the Good Die Young" by Billy Joel
"Pour Some Sugar on Me" by Def Leppard
"Purple Rain" by Prince
"Red, Red Wine" by UB-40
"She's Always a Woman to Me" by Billy Joel
"Sister Christian" by Night Ranger
"Sweet Child of Mine" by Guns 'n' Roses
"Sweet Dreams (Are Made of This)" by Eurhythmics
"Tainted Love" by Soft Cell
"Take It on the Run" by REO Speedwagon
"Take on Me" by A-Ha
"That's All" by Genesis
"Time After Time" by Cindi Lauper
"Total Eclipse of the Heart" by Bonnie Tyler
"Video Killed the Radio Star" by the Buggles
"Wake Me Up Before You Go-Go" by Wham
"The Way You Make Me Feel" by Michael Jackson
"Werewolves in London" by Warren Zevon
"You Give Love a Bad Name" by Bon Jovi
"Your Love" by the Outfield

1970s

"American Pie" by Don McLean
"Any Way You Want It" by Journey
"Babe" by Styx
"Bad, Bad Leroy Brown" by Jim Croce
"Beast of Burden" by the Rolling Stones
"Bennie and the Jets" by Elton John
"Beth" by KISS
"Bohemian Rhapsody" by Queen
"Born to Run" by Bruce Springsteen
"Brandy (You're a Fine Girl)" by the Looking Glass

"Cat's in the Cradle" by Harry Chapin
"Changes" by David Bowie
"Come Sail Away" by Styx
"Copacabana" by Barry Manilow
"Crocodile Rock" by Elton John
"Dancing Queen" by ABBA
"December 1963 (Oh, What a Night)" by Four Seasons
"Desperado" by Eagles
"Don't Stop" by Fleetwood Mac
"Dream On" by Aerosmith
"Drift Away" by Dobie Gray
"Fat Bottomed Girls" by Queen
"Heart of Gold" by Neil Young
"Horse with No Name" by America
"Hotel California" by the Eagles
"I Feel the Earth Move" by Carole King
"I Will Survive" by Gloria Gaynor
"Imagine" by John Lennon
"The Joker" by Steve Miller Band
"Joy to the World (Jerimiah)" by the Three Dog Night
"Just the Way You Are" by Billy Joel
"Layla" by Eric Clapton
"Listen to the Music" by the Doobie Brothers
"Maggie May" by Rod Stewart
"Mary Jane's Last Dance" by Tom Petty
"Maybe I'm Amazed" by Paul McCartney
"Moondance" by Van Morrison
"Old Time Rock & Roll" by Bob Seger
"Paradise by the Dashboard Light" by Meatloaf
"Piano Man" by Billy Joel
"The Piña Colada Song (Escape)" by Rupert Holmes
"Play That Funky Music White Boy" by Wild Cherry

"Rich Girl" by Hall and Oates
"Rock and Roll All Night" by KISS
"Rocket Man" by Elton John
"Running on Empty" by Jackson Browne
"Simple Man" by Lynyrd Skynyrd
"Stuck in the Middle with You" by Stealers Wheel
"Sweet Home Alabama" by Lynyrd Skynyrd
"Take It Easy" by the Eagles
"Tiny Dancer" by Elton John
"Wild World" by Cat Stevens
"Wonderful Tonight" by Eric Clapton
"Y.M.C.A." by Village People
"You Shook Me All Night Long" by AC/DC
"Your Song" by Elton John

1960s
"Bad Moon Rising" by CCR
"Blue Bayou" by Roy Orbison
"Blue Suede Shoes" by Elvis Presley
"Born to Be Wild" by Steppenwolf
"Brown Eyed Girl" by Van Morrison
"Can't Take My Eyes Off of You" by Frankie Valli
"Come Together" by the Beatles
"Daydream Believer" by the Monkees
"Delilah" by Tom Jones
"Hang on Sloopy" by the McCoys
"Happy Together" by the Turtles
"Have You Ever Seen the Rain?" by CCR
"Help Me Rhonda" by the Beach Boys
"Hey Jude" by the Beatles
"House of the Rising Sun" by the Animals
"I Saw Her Standing There" by the Beatles

"I'm a Believer" by the Monkees
"Knocking on Heaven's Door" by Bob Dylan
"Let It Be" by the Beatles
"Light My Fire" by the Doors
"The Lion Sleeps Tonight" by the Tokens
"Mrs. Robinson" by Simon and Garfunkel
"Ob-La-Di, Ob-La-Da" by the Beatles
"(Oh) Pretty Woman" by Roy Orbison
"Proud Mary" by CCR
"Runaround Sue" by Dion
"Satisfaction (I Can't Get No)" by the Rolling Stones
"Saturday in the Park" by Chicago
"Something" by the Beatles
"Sounds of Silence" by Simon and Garfunkel
"Suspicious Minds" by Elvis Presley
"Sweet Caroline" by Neil Diamond
"Twist and Shout" by the Beatles
"Unchained Melody" by the Righteous Brothers
"Viva Las Vegas" by Elvis Presley
"The Weight" by the Band
"When I'm Sixty-Four" by the Beatles
"With a Little Help from My Friends" by the Beatles
"Yesterday" by the Beatles
"Yellow Submarine" by the Beatles
"You've Lost That Loving Feeling" by the Righteous Brothers

1950s

"Ain't That a Shame" by Fats Domino
"All Shook Up" by Elvis Presley
"Blueberry Hill" by Fats Domino
"Chantilly Lace" by the Big Bopper
"Great Balls of Fire" by Jerry Lee Lewis

"Heartbreak Hotel" by Elvis Presley
"Hey Baby" by Bruce Channel
"Hound Dog" by Elvis Presley
"Jailhouse Rock" by Elvis Presley
"Johnny B. Goode" by Chuck Berry
"Kansas City" by Wilbert Harrison
"That'll Be the Day" by Buddy Holly
"Tutti Frutti" by Little Richard
"Whole Lotta Shakin' Goin' On" by Jerry Lee Lewis

Classic Motown/Soul/R & B
"Ain't No Mountain High Enough" by Marvin Gaye and Tammy Terrell
"Another Saturday Night" by Sam Cooke
"At Last" by Edda James
"Build Me Up Buttercup" by the Foundations
"Dock of the Bay" by Otis Redding
"Hit the Road Jack" by Ray Charles
"How Sweet It Is" by Junior Walker
"I Got You (I Feel Good)" by James Brown
"Lean on Me" by Bill Withers
"Let's Stay Together" by Al Green
"Mustang Sally" by Wilson Pickett
"My Girl" by Temptations
"Respect" by Aretha Franklin
"Soul Man" by Sam and Dave
"Stand by Me" by Ben E. King
"The Twist" by Chubby Checker
"Under the Boardwalk" by the Drifters

Country/Folk
"9 to 5" by Dolly Parton

"A Boy Named Sue" by Johnny Cash
"All My Ex's Live in Texas" by George Strait
"Amarillo by Morning" by George Strait
"Annie's Song" by John Denver
"Beer for My Horses" by Toby Keith and Willie Nelson
"Blue Eyes Crying in the Rain" by Willie Nelson
"Born to Boogie" by Hank Williams, Jr.
"Calling Baton Rouge "by Garth Brooks
"Chicken Fried" by Zac Brown Band
"City of New Orleans" by Arlo Guthrie
"Could I Have This Dance" by Anne Murray
"Crazy" by Patsy Cline
"The Dance" by Garth Brooks
"Devil Went Down to Georgia" by Charlie Daniels
"Dixieland Delight" by Alabama
"Family Tradition" by Hank Williams, Jr.
"Folsom Prison Blues" by Johnny Cash
"Friends in Low Places" by Garth Brooks
"Galveston" by Glen Campbell
"The Gambler" by Kenny Rogers
"God Bless the U.S.A." by Lee Greenwood
"Green, Green Grass of Home" by Tom Jones
"Hey Good Looking" by Hank Williams, Sr.
"I Love This Bar" by Toby Keith
"It's Five O'clock Somewhere" by Alan Jackson
"Jolene" by Dolly Parton
"King of the Road" by Roger Miller
"Last Date" by Floyd Cramer
"Leaving on a Jet Plane" by John Denver
"Lucille" by Kenny Rogers
"Me and Bobby McGee" by Kris Kristofferson
"Rhinestone Cowboy" by Glen Campbell

"Ring of Fire" by Johnny Cash
"Rocky Top" by Osborne Brothers
"Stand by Your Man" by Tammy Wynette
"Take Me Home Country Roads" by John Denver
"Tequila Makes Her Clothes Fall Off" by Joe Nichols
"Tennessee Whiskey" by Chris Stapleton
"Tight Fittin' Jeans" by Conway Twitty
"Wagon Wheel" by Old Crow Medicine Show
"What a Difference You've Made" by Ronnie Milsap
"You Never Even Called Me by My Name" by David Allan Coe

Island Theme/Reggae
"A Pirate Looks at Forty" by Jimmy Buffett
"Changes in Latitudes" by Jimmy Buffett
"Cheeseburger in Paradise" by Jimmy Buffett
"Fins" by Jimmy Buffett
"I Shot the Sheriff" by Bob Marley/Eric Clapton
"Knee Deep" by Zac Brown/Jimmy Buffett
"Margaritaville" by Jimmy Buffett
"Son of a Son of a Sailor" by Jimmy Buffett
"Three Little Birds" by Bob Marley
"Toes" by Zac Brown
"Where the Boat Leaves From" by Zac Brown

Pub Songs
"Danny Boy" traditional Irish
"I Like Beer" by Tom T. Hall
"The Old Dun Cow" Pub song
"Seven Drunken Nights" Pub song
"Those Were the Days" Pub song
"Unicorn" Pub song
"Wasn't That a Party?" by the Irish Rovers

"When Irish Eyes are Smiling" traditional Irish
"The Wild Rover (No, Nay, Never)" Pub song

Vocal Standards/Movies/TV/Show Tunes
"After the Lovin'"
"As Time Goes By"
"Bésame Mucho"
"The Best Is Yet to Come"
"Beyond the Sea"
"Cheers Theme"
"Close to You (They Long to Be)"
"Everybody Loves Somebody Sometime"
"Fly Me to the Moon"
"Georgia on My Mind"
"Gilligan's Island Theme"
"Girl from Ipanema"
"Greased Lightning" (from Grease)
"I Left My Heart in San Francisco"
"It Had to Be You"
"Linus and Lucy" (Peanuts theme)
"Love Boat Theme"
"Mack the Knife"
"Mister Bojangles"
"Misty"
"Moon River"
"My Way"
"New York, New York"
"One for My Baby"
"Over the Rainbow"
"Route 66"
"Summer Loving" (from Grease)
"Summer Wind"

"That's Amoré"
"Unforgettable"
"The Way You Look Tonight"
"What a Wonderful World"

Late Night/Adult Content

Depending on the cruise line or the crowd on any given night, adult-themed songs can be a lot of fun for a room full of party people or lead to sternly worded complaints from upset party poopers. These songs reside outside the category of "do no harm" because it's always possible someone in the room will be offended. Perform them judiciously and at your own risk. If I do songs in this category, I prefer cheeky over trashy, but to each their own. Add the words "piano bar" to any of the following titles when searching the internet and you'll find video demonstrating how the songs have been performed by others.

"Alice" by Smokie
"The I-95 Song" by Jimmy Buffett
"Big Balls" by AC/DC
"My Ding-a-Ling" by Chuck Berry
"Pussycat Song" by the Asylum Street Spankers
"The Rodeo Song" by David Allen Coe
"Why Don't We Get Drunk" by Jimmy Buffett

APPENDIX 4: ARRANGING SONGS

Providing you an entire study plan for the piano and arranging is beyond the scope of this book, and there is ample information available for free on the internet and specifically YouTube. But I will address a handful of concepts that are incredibly useful when creating your own arrangements of popular songs. By sharing them, I will save you months or even years trying to musically re-invent the wheel. You're welcome.

Accompaniment Patterns

If I can claim a particular style of solo piano playing, it would be that my left hand dominates. The bass patterns I employ state the genre, set the tempo, spell out the chord changes, and generally drive the song to its conclusion. I often joke that I could sit on my right hand and still get through most songs. I tend to play my bass lines lower than other pianists. This comes from using my ear and matching the octave bassists actually play in. My right hand usually hovers over middle C to play chords and seldom rises beyond the C above. If you ever see me play in person or on video you'll notice I sit with my body centered at least one octave below middle C. This is so I don't strain my wrists since I'm always playing lower on the keyboard. Personally, I find the written bass lines in piano music are just too wimpy for solo piano bar performance. By taking the left hand lower or doubling the bass line in octaves I get the driving sound that fills the room.

You do what works for you, but the following are accompaniment patterns that I use night after night and give me a starting point when creating arrangements of new additions to my repertoire. You'll notice that none of these patterns are based on the old stride style of bouncing the left hand back and forth between low notes and chords. I might do that on rare occasion as a novelty (perhaps "Crazy," "As Time Goes By," or "Last Date"), but that's about the only place it fits in contemporary piano bars. If that's your go-to style of accompaniment, you'll need to quickly add the following patterns if you want to modernize your PBE style. The notated examples are all in the key of C based on a major chord and you will need to transpose and alter the chord as needed through each song.

1. Early Rock/Boogie #1

This is a very flexible pattern I use on many songs from the 1950s and 1960s like "Great Balls of Fire," and "Tutti Frutti." It also works great on "Old Time Rock and Roll." The left hand mimics a popular blues pattern used by guitarists and the right hand spells out the chord while adding bluesy grace notes.

2. Early Rock/Boogie #2

The right hand mostly stays out of the way on this one. You can really play any simple chord pattern you want and put your attention on the left hand. If your chord is a triad of only three notes, I typically double the root or the fifth to beef up the sound. This pattern works great on rockers like "Little Sister" and "Stuck in the Middle" or country tunes like "Boot Scoot 'n' Boogie" and "Jackson."

3. Jump Swing

Again, this pattern is mostly all about the left hand. As the chords move around, keep the left hand in the lower octaves to sound more like a bassist than a pianist. The chord inversions you play in the right hand don't really matter; just keep the upbeat rhythm going. If you're not sure how to play with a swing feel, do an internet search for the difference between even and swing 8th notes and you'll find plenty of excellent tutorials. This is a great pattern for older swing songs like "All Shook Up," "Kansas City," and "King of the Road."

4. The Two-step

This is probably the simplest and most used of all the accompaniment patterns. It is incredibly flexible and can be used for old jazz ballads, adult-contemporary pop songs, and slow or mid-tempo rock songs. The point of this pattern is to mostly stay out of the way and simply provide subtle rhythmic and harmonic support for the vocal melody. The right hand could play a thousand variations on what I provide here, but keep it simple with sustained chords or the occasional rolling arpeggio. The left hand just moves casually from the root to the 5th of each chord. If the chord only lasts a couple beats, you'll only have time for the root. Keep in mind that this pattern, and most of the others presented here, work for both even 8th note or shuffle/swing rhythms. All you need to do is adjust the timing of the 8th notes in the left hand. Just a few of the thousands of songs this pattern works for include "Friends in Low Places," "Your Song," "All My Exes Live in Texas," "Misty," and "Sweet Caroline."

5. The Rhumba/Cha-cha

This pattern has a fairly basic left hand that moves from the root to the fifth. It's the right hand that keeps things going. The exact inversion of the chord doesn't matter. It's all about the rhythm. If the chord is a triad, the bottom note is doubled at the octave because the pattern needs four notes. I use this pattern several times a night on songs from many decades. Some examples include; "Margaritaville," "Tequila Sunrise," "Blue Bayou," "Stand by Me," "It's Now or Never," and "Toes" from the Zac Brown Band.

6. The Bossa Nova

The bass line for the Bossa Nova is the same as the Rhumba pattern. The difference comes from the pattern in the right hand that mimics a clavé rhythm. Inversions of the chord don't matter as long as you play legato (smooth and connected) and keep the rhythm going. The Bossa Nova is not much in style anymore, but I still get enough requests to mention it. Some examples include, "Girl from Ipanema" and "Night and Day."

7. Basic Rock

The bass line of basic rock pattern is just like the two-step or Bossa Nova except you stay on the root of the chord rather than alternate to the 5th. Because it's so simple, the pattern can be used in a variety of styles and tempos. I often double the lower bass note at the octave or let it sustain as in the notated example. Either option beefs up the sound. For the right hand, think like a guitar player and emulate an easy going strumming pattern. Pretty much anything that adds a little rhythm and harmony but stays out of the way is going to work. Just a few of the thousands of songs this pattern applies to are "Desperado," "Summer of '69," "Hey Jude," "Dock of the Bay," "American Pie," and "Mr. Brightside."

8. Hip-hop/Contemporary R & B

Hip-hop is one of the most difficult styles to emulate on piano because the songs are often based on rhythmic grooves without definitive bass lines and chord changes. The emphasis is on the delivery of the words and a beat rather than conventional songwriting. But there are guests who request hip-hop, so what do you do? My solution has been to borrow from what others have already done. Go to a dueling piano bar and see what those performers have come up with. If that isn't feasible, do a search on YouTube for a song you're interested in but add the words "piano bar." Chances are, someone else has figured out a way to play that song on solo piano and a video has found its way online. I've used both of these suggestions for songs like, "Baby Got Back," "No Diggity," and "Gin and Juice." I won't provide a notated example for this category because there are just too many possibilities. Listen to what others have done and borrow/steal what sounds good.

9. Traditional and Jazz Waltzes

Very few people know how to dance to a waltz, but I still get requested to play them regularly. The traditional waltz (measures 1-2 of the example) is very rigid but still has its use. The left hand alternates between the root and 5th while the right chops away at any inversion of the chord that is handy. Songs that use a traditional waltz pattern include "Can I Have This Dance" "Lucile," "Delilah," "That's Amoré," and "Piano Man." The jazz waltz (measures 3-4 of the example) uses the same notes in the left hand but is more rhythmically interesting. The 8th-notes should have a swing feel to propel the rhythm forward. Jazz waltzes include "My Favorite Things," and "Someday My Prince Will Come."

10. Slow 12/8

The slow 12/8 pattern makes an appearance most every night I perform. The left hand is similar to the basic rock pattern while the right hand carries the load with rolling arpeggios. If the chord is a triad, double the bottom note one octave higher. Whenever the chords change, move to the nearest inversion so the rolling pattern stays smooth. Songs that use this pattern include "Can't Help Falling in Love," "House of the Rising Sun," "Colour My World," and "What a Wonderful World."

11. Reggae/Island

Because many cruises sail to exotic tropical or island destinations, songs with Reggae rhythms are very popular with guests. There can be considerable variety in the bass line, but the upbeat pulse in the right hand is common to most Reggae rhythms. When in doubt, simplify the bass, but keep that right hand bubbling along. Reggae songs include "Three Little Birds," "Red, Red Wine," "Wild World," and "I Shot the Sherriff."

12. Riff-based Songs

The are many great songs based on riffs instead of accompaniment patterns. Riffs are usually lines of single notes with a very identifiable and repetitive hook. There are also songs, like "Lean on Me," Louie Louie," or "December 1963" where the riff is based on a chord progression. The easy thing about riff-based songs is that you don't need to wonder what accompaniment pattern to use. It's all about learning the riff. The trouble comes if the riff is rhythmically challenging or doesn't lend itself to piano very well. A trick I use to get around that problem is to play the riff during an introduction so everyone knows what song I'm performing, but when the vocals start I switch to a more relaxed accompaniment pattern. For example, I do this with "You Shook Me All Night Long" from AC/DC. Remember, the main sections of a song guests are interested in is the introduction so they can decide how much they already love the song and the chorus where they can sing along. Everything else is potentially nothing more than filler. Some riff-based songs include "Play That Funky Music White Boy," "Superstition," "Paradise City," "Walk This Way," or "Back in Black." Some songs, like "Satisfaction" or "Living on a Prayer" are riff based for only some of the song and use standard rock patterns the rest of the time.

A Note on Ending a Song

Song endings are a pet peeve of mine. There's nothing that ruins an otherwise decent rendition of a song for me than a wimpy ending that sounds unprepared if not apologetic. It telegraphs to the listener that you're not on top of your game. Have you ever attended a music recital for kids and notice how they immediately scurry away from the piano the moment they hit the last note? It's like they can't wait to get away from the scene of the crime. Well you're an adult, so don't be like that. You're a musician, not a criminal.

Many songs you'll play don't have endings on the original recordings because they fade out, so you'll have to create your own. One suggestion is to find videos online of the artist performing live and copy that ending. If you have to create an ending from scratch, there are several tactics you can try. Build up to it by repeating the last phrase a few times. Or try doing a grand ritard with a pregnant pause just before the last chord. Or end by dropping the accompaniment and going a cappella (I do this often with "Rocket Man" from Elton John or "Hallelujah" from Leonard Cohen and people enjoy the sentimental feel of it). For a dramatic ending, play a rising arpeggio followed by a glissando down to a loud, rumbling chord and let it ring. Guests will forgive a multitude of musical sins if you simply smile your way through a song and conclude with a well-conceived ending that says, "I have pride in what I just played for you."

APPENDIX 5: LEARNING SONGS

If you remember way back in the introduction of this book, you read that one cruise line expects you to know 250 popular songs in order to be hired by them. That's certainly a good number to aim for if you are a first-time PBE, but don't stop there. Learn another 250, and another 250, and another. Using a tablet on stage means you don't have to memorize the chords and lyrics to every song, and that's a good thing. You just need enough familiarity that if you can take a few peeks at the song sheet on your screen you'll be able to get through the performance with confidence. The more songs you know, the more tips you'll make—the correlation is quite simple.

I will also point out that if you're working 6-7 nights a week for months at a time, knowing "only" 250 songs will become painfully boring. Learning new material keeps you engaged with your job and feeling like a pro-active musician. And lastly, since performing songs is what gives you pleasure in life, more songs in your repertoire means more personal satisfaction, and that's important towards maintaining a positive state of mind over the long term. I've slowed my pace these days but still learn 100 songs per year just to stay sharp. I added five more just this week.

I gave you an expansive list songs you should perform in Chapter 1 and Appendix 3, so now let's focus on an efficient way to learn those suggestions.

What Songs to Learn First

If you haven't already, learn the Big-10 and all 50 songs from Chapter 1 first. Those are your fail-safe songs that will be heavily requested. Beyond those songs, start working your way through the expanded list in Appendix 3 as well as other songs you personally enjoy playing. Guests who often frequent piano bars will appreciate hearing the occasional "special" song that sets you apart from other PBEs they've heard.

When guests request songs I don't already know, I ask myself one of two questions, "Is this a good song I've heard many times but just haven't gotten to yet?" or "Is this a song I've never really heard, but I've gotten multiple requests for it?" If the answer is yes to either question, it's probably time to learn that song. A song I've grown up hearing is usually much quicker to learn. Often, as soon as I find the lyrics and chords symbols online I'm able to perform the song without practicing it. But with songs that are new to me, I ultimately consider what my ROI (return on investment) will be if I spend the extra time learning it. Most the time it's worth it because guests are giving me good suggestions and it's not unusual to receive a $20 tip when I play it for them a few nights later (one guess tipped me $400 for learning a rather obscure J.J. Cale song called "Magnolia"). But there are a handful of songs that have been requested several times, and I've simply decided, "no, that one isn't for me." If the guest asks about it, I politely say, "I didn't have time to learn it, but here's another song I think you'll like," and move on.

Operating Procedure for Learning Songs

I'll walk you through what works for me to learn songs and you can adjust the process as needed. This isn't a one-size-fits-all procedure because some songs are easier to learn than others based on your previous familiarity and the song's inherent technical difficulties, but it's a good place to start.

Get the Lyrics and Chords: I normally start my search at Ultimate Guitar (https://www.ultimate-guitar.com/), but typing the title of the song plus "lyrics and chords" into a search engine will give you other options. Popular songs may have several renditions submitted by users, so I usually pick the one with the highest rating. Then, I copy the text from the web page into a Word doc template. I have found that what works best for me is a song sheet in all bold, using Ariel font with the lyrics in black and the chord symbols in red. The lyrics are double-spaced with the chords on the spaces between. The font size ranges from 12-16 point based on what fits on a single page.

Acquire the Recording: If I am at home with strong internet, I usually find the song on YouTube. On a ship, video streaming doesn't usually work, so I download the file from iTunes or elsewhere on days I have a phone signal.

Verify the Lyrics: since the lyrics in your song sheet came from a crowd-sourced website, you'll want to verify they are correct. You will find that people often repeat the text for each occurrence of the chorus. I delete those portions and insert the words "repeat chorus." This saves space and makes it easier to fit the entire song on one page.

Edit the Chords Symbols: start listening carefully to the recording for where the chords change. I usually tune in to the bass instrument for the most clarity, then scoot the chord symbols over the exact words where they change. Along the way, I check the chords on a keyboard to see if I like them. Crowd-sourced chord symbols are often wrong so don't think twice about changing them if you hear something peculiar.

Transpose as Needed: I know my vocal range well enough that I can usually tell right away what key I will need to transpose a new song to. Listen through the entire song for the highest vocal note. How many steps away from that note is your comfortable highest note? That tells you how far you need to transpose. And even if you can hit that high note, ask yourself if you want to be doing it night after night for weeks at a time. There's no shame in bringing it down. Guests are not deducting points for each half step. Even superstar artists are transposing songs down as they age so it's no big deal for you doing it. Once you decide on a key, you'll need to adjust all the chord symbols in your song sheet accordingly. This is one reason it's helpful to understand basic music theory.

Insert Notated Passages: if the song has a very identifiable introduction (for example, "Your Song" from Elton John or "Don't Stop Believing" from Journey) or interlude ("Africa" from Toto or "In My Life" from the Beatles), you might want the passage notated so you'll remember it when you go months between performances. If you don't already own the sheet music, search for the name of the song on the internet and add the words "sheet music." You'll see several images of the first page of the sheet music you can review for free. Enter these measures into Finale (or pay someone to do it for you) and transpose them to the key you need. Unless the bass clef is very important, I only enter the treble clef and add the chord symbols above, essentially creating a short lead sheet. Those measures can then be saved as an image file and inserted into the song sheet at the appropriate location.

Import to Your Tablet: for me, this means saving the Word document as a PDF and importing it to my iPad app through Dropbox (when I have internet) or iTunes file sharing (when I'm on a ship). The app you use may allow for different file types and importing options.

Create an Accompaniment: you've played piano long enough to know there is no replacement for "bench time" when it comes to learning a new song. Open the song sheet on your tablet, sit at your keyboard, and start doing the work you know has to be done. Start by classifying the rhythmic feel or genre of the song. Is it medium rock? Latin based? Have a swing feel? A country two-step? If so, use one of my accompaniment patterns from Appendix 4 and see if it works. Mixing and matching is also allowed. For example, try using the left hand of the two-step pattern with the right hand of the Rhumba pattern (I do that for "Brown-eyed Girl"). It's not important that you re-create a spot-on rendition of the original recording. It's more like an impressionistic version than a literal copy. Guests are perfectly happy hearing your interpretation of a song. Remember, the fact that you can play and sing songs at all is enough to impress most guests. You just need to create an accompaniment that is smooth, keeps the beat, and gives you a basic foundation to present the melody (your voice) over.

Fix the Mistakes and Practice: plan on the first couple drafts of a song sheet to have errors. Sometimes this includes the key just not being a good fit. The app I have allows markings to be inserted into the file, so I circle the mistakes as I find them and then go back to my computer for corrections. If I don't do it this way, I nearly always forget what the mistakes were by the time I open the original Word document. I check the improvements and run the song a few more times if it's new to me. If it's song I am strongly familiar with, I may be ready to perform with only one run-through (or not at all). But it never fails that the first time I perform a song in front of a crowd is when I realize what parts of it need more work. It could be the vocal phrasing, where to breathe, tweaking the vowel sounds, or perhaps the accompaniment is getting in my way, and I need to work on it separately (the answer is usually to simplify it). After performing the song to an audience a couple times, I consider the song "learned," add it to my master song list, and move on to the next one. It never ends.

Here is an example of "Happy Birthday" in song sheet form. Using this song avoids any copyright issues because it is now confirmed to be in the public domain. After playing the introduction in lead-sheet form, I use a traditional waltz pattern and change chords based on the symbols above the words as I sing them.

HOW TO BE AN AWESOME PIANO BAR ENTERTAINER ON CRUISE SHIPS

    F   C7
Happy birthday to you
    C7   F
Happy birthday to you
    F   Bb
Happy birthday dear [insert name]
    F   C7 F
Happy birthday to you

Here is an image of the accompaniment I might play completely notated. This is just for a reference so you can see the "before and after." Sometimes I skip the intro and enter straight away with the vocals.

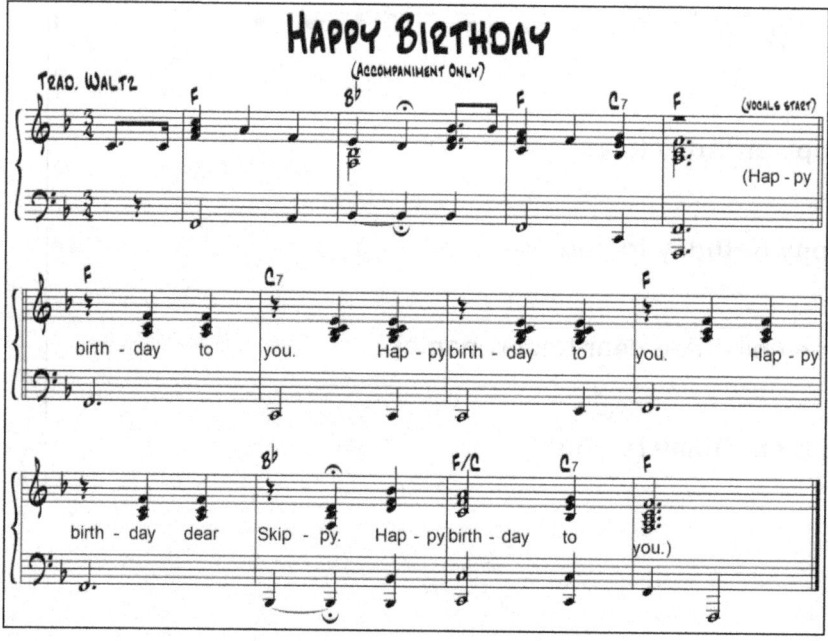

ABOUT THE AUTHOR

Dr. Gregg Akkerman was born in the southern California desert to a mother with the good sense to provide her son the same birthday as Duke Ellington. He worked many years as a pianist/vocalist throughout the Southwest before earning a Masters of Music in Jazz Studies from San Diego State University and a Doctorate of Arts in Music Theory and Composition from the University of Northern Colorado. His recent books include *Experiencing Led Zeppelin*, and he was the founding editor of *The Listener's Companion* series from Rowman and Littlefield. After teaching for a decade as an Associate Professor of Music, Akkerman returned to California to further his career as a piano bar entertainer.

Author Gregg Akkerman
(photo by Don Emmanuel de Vera)

REVIEW REQUEST

If you enjoyed this book and found it useful, I'd be very grateful if you'd post an honest review. Your support matters as I do read all the reviews and make changes based on your feedback.

If you'd like to leave a review, all you need to do is go to the book's Amazon page. In the Customer Review area you'll see a button/link that says "Write a customer review" – click on that and you're good to go.

Thank you for the support,
Gregg

Click here or on the book cover image to leave a review!

OTHER BOOKS FROM GREGG AKKERMAN

<u>The Keyboardist's Career Guide:</u> A 10-Step Plan to Your Dream Job in the Music Business

JUST FOR KEYBOARDISTS! This first-of-its-kind career guide delivers a proven path for players of all abilities to make a living in the music business. You'll find 50+ career options with specific details, a 10-step plan to professional success, clear timelines for making at least $5,000 a month, and dozens of PROTIPS on the business of being a keyboardist.

So Good, So Good, So Good! Confessions of the Piano Dude:
A Memoir of Cruise Ship Life, Serial Rapists, Becoming Minimalist, Finding Love, and Living the Dream

Serial rapists. Celebrities. Naked people. Jail. And then some weird stuff happened too!

Just another day on the job for the Piano Dude. **Gregg Akkerman's** life as an entertainer reads like a **Cohen brothers-meets-Jimmy-Buffett** screenplay that never ends. Is it really just one Caribbean island and piano bar full of bizarre characters after another? Skinny dipping with 6-time Grammy winners? An awkward chat with Bill Cosby? It's all in this book. Whether you're a cruising enthusiast, piano-bar junkie, musician, or reader of quirky "I wonder if that really happened" memoires, you'll find a **page-turning winner** that is "So Good."

Experiencing Led Zeppelin: A Listener's Companion

Consider Akkerman the voice of expert knowledge whispering in your ear as you listen to the music of hard rock's greatest band. Every song in the Led Zeppelin studio-record catalog is discussed.

From "Black Dog," to "Stairway to Heaven," and "Whole Lotta Love," it's all here.

The Last Balladeer: The Johnny Hartman Story

You've heard Hartman's glorious baritone voice on the iconic *John Coltrane and Johnny Hartman* album as well as in Clint Eastwood's *Bridges of Madison County* movie, and now you can read Akkerman's exquisitely written biography about the balladeer's life and music.

Made in the USA
Middletown, DE
07 June 2024

55421414R00089